The Ultimate Guide to Doing a PhD

The Ultimate Guide to Doing a PhD

Merle van den Akker, PhD

 World Scientific

NEW JERSEY · LONDON · SINGAPORE · BEIJING · SHANGHAI · HONG KONG · TAIPEI · CHENNAI · TOKYO

Published by

World Scientific Publishing Europe Ltd.

57 Shelton Street, Covent Garden, London WC2H 9HE

Head office: 5 Toh Tuck Link, Singapore 596224

USA office: 27 Warren Street, Suite 401-402, Hackensack, NJ 07601

Library of Congress Cataloging-in-Publication Data
Names: Akker, Merle van den, author.
Title: The ultimate guide to doing a PhD / Merle van den Akker.
Description: London : World Scientific, 2023.
Identifiers: LCCN 2022045049 | ISBN 9781800613454 (hardcover) |
  ISBN 9781800613645 (paperback) | ISBN 9781800613461 (ebook) |
  ISBN 9781800613478 (ebook other)
Subjects: LCSH: Doctor of philosophy degree--Handbooks, manuals, etc. | Graduate students--
  Handbooks, manuals, etc. | Universities and colleges--Graduate work--Handbooks, manuals, etc. |
  Study skills--Handbooks, manuals, etc.
Classification: LCC LB2386 .A44 2023 | DDC 378.2--dc23/eng/20221103
LC record available at https://lccn.loc.gov/2022045049

British Library Cataloguing-in-Publication Data
A catalogue record for this book is available from the British Library.

Copyright © 2023 by World Scientific Publishing Europe Ltd.

All rights reserved. This book, or parts thereof, may not be reproduced in any form or by any means, electronic or mechanical, including photocopying, recording or any information storage and retrieval system now known or to be invented, without written permission from the Publisher.

For photocopying of material in this volume, please pay a copying fee through the Copyright Clearance Center, Inc., 222 Rosewood Drive, Danvers, MA 01923, USA. In this case permission to photocopy is not required from the publisher.

For any available supplementary material, please visit
https://www.worldscientific.com/worldscibooks/10.1142/Q0397#t=suppl

Desk Editors: Jayanthi Muthuswamy/Adam Binnie/Shi Ying Koe

Typeset by Stallion Press
Email: enquiries@stallionpress.com

I dedicate this book to all PhD students: past, present and future.

To those who've gone before, like David. To those who're currently in it, like Amy. And to those who might eventually take the plunge, like Seb.

About the Author

Merle van den Akker, PhD, was a PhD student at the time of writing this book. She studied the effect of different payment methods on personal finance management at the Warwick Business School. As this book went into publication, Merle has finished her PhD and now proudly calls herself Dr van den Akker. She has left academia and has become a behavioral science manager at a financial well-being unit in an Australian bank. She continues to study and apply behavioral science to improve financial services and consumer (financial) well-being.

During her PhD, Merle started the blog Money on the Mind, where she blogged about behavioral science, personal finance, as well as her experiences during the PhD journey. The former two topics have made Merle a sought-after speaker and researcher on the intersection of behavioral science and personal finance (which majorly helped land her a job outside of academia after the PhD). The latter, her writing on her PhD experiences, have led to an enormous amount of people reaching out, and one-on-one interactions that made her realize that there was a dire need for a guide to help out PhD students, through each and every stage of the PhD process. This book is the result of that.

Acknowledgments

It took me a while to write this book. The main struggles were finishing my PhD and transitioning out of academia, as well as just making sure this book was actually complete and helpful.

First, I have to thank my amazing PhD cohort; it's due to their honesty that some chapters in this book even exist. A special mention to Lara, my closest friend and colleague in the cohort. Without her, it would have been an absolute nightmare. Not in my actual PhD cohort but an invaluable colleague, friend, advisor and soundboard is David. Thank you for pulling me through both the PhD and the writing of this book.

Second is the unconditional yet critical support of friends, whether they knew what a PhD entailed, or what writing a book entailed, or neither. Amy, Pauline, James and Seb, I will always continue to be thankful for your support and listening ears and apologetic for how long I can go on about a topic that is barely of interest to you.

And last, of course, the parents. Mom, dad, you have been my absolute rock throughout the process of doing the PhD. I'm forever amazed by your faith in me and will always strive to do you proud.

This book is a result of all the amazing people in my life. And you'll need amazing people to make it to the end of a PhD.

Contents

About the Author   vii

Acknowledgments   ix

Introduction   xv

Section 1   Should You Do a PhD?   **1**

1   Reasons to NOT Do a PhD   5

2   A Critical Evaluation of Reasons to Do a PhD   11

3   The Practicalities of Doing a PhD   17

4   Biggest Misconceptions of Doing a PhD   23

5   So Should You Do a PhD?   31

Section 2   Applying to the PhD   **33**

6   Finding a Topic   37

7   Finding a University   41

8   Finding a Supervisor   43

9   Finding Funding   49

10   Getting Your Documents in Order   55

11	How to Survive an Interview	59
12	Offers and Rejections	61
13	Concluding Remarks	65

Section 3 Starting the PhD! — 67

14	Settling in	71
15	Coursework	75
16	Planning the Research	79
17	My Supervisor and I	83
18	First-Year PhD Review	91
19	Concluding Remarks	97

Section 4 Getting on with the PhD! — 99

20	Structure Amidst Chaos	103
21	Teaching	109
22	Conferences	113
23	Writing It All Down	119
24	The Publication Journey	125
25	Time Management and Multi-Tasking	131
26	Taking Breaks	137
27	Mental Health	141
28	Failure	151
29	Talking Supervisors (Again)	159
30	What Do You Want from the PhD?	167
31	Mentoring	175
32	Knowing When to Quit	179

33	Doing a PhD Is Not Enough	187
34	PhD Review, Year 2	191
35	PhD Review, Year 3	197
36	Concluding Remarks	203

Section 5   Finishing the PhD — **205**

37	Balancing the PhD with the Job Hunt	209
38	Leveraging Contacts	215
39	Mental Health Revisited	217
40	A Good PhD Is a Finished PhD	223
41	Submission!	227
42	Final-Year PhD Review	229
43	Things I Would Have Done Differently	237
44	Concluding Remarks	243

Section 6   PhDone! Now What? — **245**

45	The Anti-Climax of Submitting	249
46	The Break?!	253
47	The Viva	257
48	Concluding Remarks: The Aftermath	263

Conclusion — 265

Introduction

Hi, I'm Merle. And as I'm writing this book, I'm a PhD student in the UK, conducting research into how different payment methods affect how people spend, manage and relate to money. By the time this book is out, I'll have finished the PhD. Wow! And because clearly I'm now an *expert* at doing a PhD, I thought I'd share some advice.

All jokes about me being an expert aside, I did write this book to help. When I decided to do a PhD and even during a lot of the PhD, I had no real clue as to what I was doing or to what I should be doing. And I would have really enjoyed a resource like this.

I'm clearly not the only person who would've enjoyed such a resource. I started blogging in the summer of 2018. My blog, Money on the Mind, initially focused on behavioral science and personal finance, as that is my work and my main topic of interest. However, on the side, I also blogged about my PhD experience, and that made some waves.

It wasn't long until I had people reach out to me for help. And when I say it wasn't long, I mean I had barely published five posts on the topic. Questions were quite broad. They ranged from "how do I choose the right PhD?" to "I'm not sure about what to do after I finish the PhD". By this stage, I think I've seen, and tried to help, with most questions.

But because these often were one-on-one conversations, the economies of scale of my *world-renowned* advice were actually terrible. I continued combatting this issue by blogging more about my experience and every question I received regarding the PhD, but quite frankly, after a while, you simply can't keep up. As a result, I decided to write a book. Because I love writing and because you love having useful information stored in a single, easy-to-access location. It's a win–win.

So I wrote this book to help. In this book, I'll go through the most frequently asked questions, try to debunk some serious misconceptions, elaborate on my own experiences and mistakes and try to establish as accurately a picture of the whole PhD process as humanly possible. And I do mean the whole process.

We are going to start at the very beginning: the inception of the idea of maybe doing a PhD. Should you? Can you? Do you really need to? These are some key questions to start off with. From thereon, if you have realized that your desire to do a PhD stems from the core of your very being, I'll dive into the practicalities of choosing PhD programs, supervisors, funding schemes and the whole lot and how to properly apply to them. Don't make the mistake of taking these processes lightly. They are time consuming, demotivating and often disappointing. But more about that later!

And once you have received your golden ticket, the offer to become a PhD student, the fun really begins. And I will have loads of tips here too because there is a lot more to learn! Expectation management, communication, time management, mental health, networking and future career prospects are just a few topics that come to mind when discussing how to do a PhD. Don't worry, there are many more topics to discuss. I mean, this is the *ultimate* guide to doing a PhD after all.

I hope that this book can help and support or at least explain and normalize some of the stuff that goes on in a PhD program. That's the best-case scenario. Worst-case scenario, I'll just have told you every mistake my friends and I made, so you can recognize and hopefully avoid them. Here's hoping!

Section 1

Should You Do a PhD?

It might sound like a rather odd question given that you've picked up this book. I feel like you might have asked yourself this question already. Several times. You'll probably have discussed with others as well. You may even be so prepared as to have had this discussion with potential supervisors and have reached out to those already in a PhD program to see if it's the right fit for you.

But even then, I ask you to contemplate this again: "should you do a PhD?"

Like I said, I'm sure you've asked yourself this question already, but I would really, and I do mean REALLY, like to emphasize that deciding to do a PhD is *serious business*.

The reason the PhD is such *serious business* is that it comes at a massive, what economists call, opportunity cost. Without too much jargon, an opportunity cost is the cost of all the other things that you could be doing with your resources during the duration of the PhD. When I say resources, I predominantly mean time, money and attention (or cognitive effort, if you prefer).

If you're committing yourself to doing a PhD, that is a 3-to-7-year commitment. The reason the year range is so wide on this commitment depends on where and in what field you're doing the PhD. PhDs in the US easily take 6 years, because they have integrated training (essentially a master's degree) in the first 2 years of the program. This is also true for the field of economics, where the training is also integrated (MRes). In the

UK, a program can be as short as 3 years, where there is no integrated training at all, and funding (the money you're being paid to do research) simply stops after those 36 months.

Whichever program duration you happen to find yourself in, what I'm trying to say, in a rather "beating around the bush" type of way, is that 3 years is a long time. And 7 years is an even longer time. There are many other things that you can do in that time. Trust me, I've had many visions of the things I could be doing with my time had I not done a PhD. These visions come to me particularly often when I've had an especially rough day. Or month.

Anyway, without much further ado, I think the best way of going about this is to first dive into reasons to not do a PhD, second, to look at reasons often cited for doing a PhD and whether they're any good and, last, to dispel some serious misconceptions!

Reasons to NOT Do a PhD

When I initially wrote the blogpost "Why you *shouldn't* do a PhD", it was my 14th article on the topic of doing a PhD. I published it on the 26th of August, 2019, which meant that by this stage, I was about to finish the second year of my PhD program (mine was 4 years total).

To promote my blogposts talking about the PhD, I followed several hashtags and accounts on Twitter focusing exclusively on the several stages of academia, most notably the PhD. I can really recommend @AcademicChatter, #PhD, #phdchat and #AcademicTwitter. It was on the latter that a tweet with #PhD was retweeted and gained a lot of traction. The tweet went as follows:

OK. It's happening, and I can finally talk openly about it (a thread). I have decided to transfer from my #PhD into a #Masters degree. I'm currently writing my thesis — I'm due to submit in October. And I want to talk about it, because we don't talk about this enough.

Tweets like these are heart-wrenching. The decision to terminate a PhD is a very serious one. Arguably, a more serious one than even starting the PhD.

Also, this wasn't one tweet. This was an 11-tweet thread, explaining the thought process(es) behind the decision to switch back to a master's degree. Apparently, quitting a PhD is so controversial; it needs 11 times 280 characters. And this tweet has been liked, commented on and retweeted several times. So, it obviously resonates.

The fact that this tweet resonated did not surprise me. I wouldn't even be surprised if this tweet from the 25th of July, 2019 would resonate even more now. The reason for this being that participation in PhD programs is becoming increasingly popular as a result of the commercialization of education. But more on that later.

It was this tweet and my annual PhD reviews which I have written for the blog that got me into thinking about certain characteristics, contexts and circumstances in which I would very much urge you NOT to do a PhD. And because this is so undervalued and underrepresented in academia, I'll just write about it myself.

We will start with absolutely terrible reasons to do a PhD. Reasons that even from the get-go just make you go "No".

Continuing a PhD requires a lot of effort, motivation and discipline. These reasons do not help out with any of those requirements. So, I wouldn't advise banking on them.

These reasons would be something like the following:

1. you didn't know what else to do;
2. you just want to be a Dr;
3. your family expects you to;
4. everyone else seems to be doing it.

1. You didn't know what else to do

Remember when I mentioned opportunity costs? Good. That is the core of this section. Not knowing what else to do besides a PhD is a terrible reason for doing a PhD. Why? Because it indicates you having done no research whatsoever, the PhD just having come on your way, and you simply taking it because it's there.

Also, it rather indicates a complete lack of interest in your future. Why are you not doing more research into what you want to do? Are you really sure you want to commit 3 to 7 years of your life to a PhD? Do you know what this entails? Are you sure there's nothing else you'd rather do in the upcoming 3 to 7 years? Have you asked yourself any of these questions at all? Do you care?!

Now I might seem a bit heated, and quite frankly, I am. There are lots of people with great motivations for doing a PhD, who've looked forward to that opportunity for a long time and have prepared accordingly.

They should not have to compete against people who happen to vaguely know what a PhD is about and are so-so about it.

Additionally, getting into a PhD because you had no clue what else was out there often signals that you're not entirely sure about what a PhD entails. This is actually a pretty decent indicator of dropping out. If you have no clue what you're in for, everything is going to be a surprise and not necessarily a positive one. More on this in Chapter 4.

If you have done active research throughout the whole market, have looked at all (well let's say most or at least a lot of) your options and the PhD turns out to be the most appealing one, well, in that case, go for it. But do your research!

2. You just want to be a Dr

It's a sexy title, I'll give you that. But is that worth 3 to 7 years of your life? I think a lot of people underestimate how much work a PhD is. And I don't think it's getting easier as the years go by. I've had several talks with my supervisor where he claims that the PhD was a great time, where he was in the pub often, was really relaxed and producing and publishing high-quality research was quite easy. I can promise you now, this is not the experience that most current PhD students have.

A PhD is a lot of hard work, against very little to no immediate reward or positive feedback (again, more on this in Chapters 4, 27 and 39). The rate of mental health issues, predominantly depression and anxiety, is incredibly high among PhD students. A lot of people work longer hours than the standard 40-hour work week and work all hours of the day, as they are completely engrossed in their work. There are obviously exceptions to this, but because of the flexibility of the PhD, there aren't as many boundaries in place.

I can keep this section relatively short: wanting to be a Dr is not enough motivation to get you through 3 to 7 years of hard work. You wouldn't push yourself through years of studying medicine just for that title either, would you?

3. Your family expects you to

Now, this is a bit of an odd one, but granted, it does happen. If there is a longstanding family tradition of obtaining PhD degrees, or you are the first in your family to even attend university and there is the (perceived) pressure of going *all the way*, well, that can go really badly.

If this expectation is one that you can live with, i.e. you were aware of this expectation and have shaped your own desires for the future accordingly, I don't think it is too much of an issue. But this rather obviously assumes that you have an intrinsic motivation for doing the PhD yourself, and your family has simply helped shape this motivation.

If the motivation is entirely extrinsic, i.e. your family is pushing you into a PhD, and that prospect is not remotely in line with your desires for the future, we're going to have a problem. If you really don't want to do a PhD, you're going to have to tell your family eventually. Now, I don't recommend starting a screaming match, but coming to the table prepared, with logical arguments for why you shouldn't do a PhD and, most alternatively, what the value is of doing something else.

When presenting your alternative career paths, frame them in such a way that appeals to your family. For this, you'll need to figure out why it is that your family wants you to do a PhD so badly. Is it status? Because that can be obtained in many different ways. Is it job security? Because I'm sure it won't take much research to show that job security in the academic sector is terrible during the first 20 years or so. Is it money? Same issue as the previous statement. I'm sure after presenting your family with a good argument of the current state of academia and the appeal of alternatives, they might come around.

And in the end, getting into a PhD, the actual application process, is long and arduous. You could just simply not do it!

4. Everyone else seems to be doing it

I can promise you, the majority of people are definitely not enrolled in PhD programs.

Academia is very much a bubble. Being at a university, especially if you live on its campus as well and don't interact much with non-university goers, can really skew your perception of what's going on in the world and what your role in that should be.

I'm sure that if you're enrolled in a very theoretical master's degree, there's quite a large subset of your fellow students who are considering and applying to PhD programs. This is not surprising. However, keep in mind that this is a very small and specific subset of people. They are by no means representative of society or the population as a whole.

It can be difficult to look outside your bubble and see what other people are doing with their lives. This actually ties in with point 1 really well. Just because everyone else is doing it doesn't mean it's the only option out there. And it definitely doesn't mean it's the only option for you. Do your research. Find what works for you. And if that ends up going against the grain, well, so be it.

Keep in mind that there's a large opportunity cost associated with doing things you don't want to do. It's 3 to 7 years of your life after all.

A Critical Evaluation of Reasons to Do a PhD

If, after reading the previous chapter, you're still thinking of doing a PhD, well, that's great. Glad we got the first hurdle out of the way. Now, let's look at the second hurdle. We have established terrible reasons to do a PhD, but now we need to dive deeper. So, ask yourself why?

Can you come up with an active reason for why you want to do the PhD (that's not from the previous chapter)? If you cannot come up with a proper reason, maybe think of a plan B.

Now, there are plenty of good reasons to do a PhD:

1. you want to be an academic;
2. you want to continue working in research;
3. a PhD will give you a large advantage in the job market;
4. you have a keen interest in studying a specific topic/project.

These four seem to be the ones most often mentioned when it comes to doing a PhD. And they don't seem like bad reasons at first, it's just that maybe we should be slightly more critical of them.

1. You want to be an academic

Surprisingly enough, there are other ways into academia than doing a PhD. Let me present some of them here. From a master's degree onwards, you can hold positions such as Research Fellow and Teaching Fellow.

These are, believe it or not, academic positions. I only became aware of these positions months after having started my PhD. They can, sometimes, be applied to by people who do not hold a PhD degree. However, as the market becomes more and more competitive and more people hold PhDs, this might not be your best bet as a starting point for working your way up the ladder.

A slightly more successful strategy, albeit one that is really Machiavellian in duration, is to go into business first. The success of this strategy rather depends on how the academic side of your field looks at its business counterpart, but often, universities do hire titans from industry into their programs, as academic staff. The reason for this is quite simple: a lot of people studying that field will actually move into industry, and having a professor with a lot of practical experience can teach students valuable business insights, which is something a lot of "pure" academics simply cannot do. It also attracts a lot of people to the program of study in question and is a great marketing tactic.

Before worrying about having to become a titan in business, you don't have to become super successful for this workout. Many companies collaborate with academic institutions, and several of those long-term collaborators find themselves working more and more in academia, holding part-time lecturing and teaching positions. So, you can ease into it, from a business perspective.

Now, I know these alternative strategies aren't exactly for everyone either, especially not if you want to be an academic and nothing but an academic. But keep in mind, the academic process isn't that quick either. And a PhD won't guarantee a post-doc position or a position in academia in general. And a post-doc won't guarantee you an assistant or associate professor position, and from thereon, there is also no certainty that you'll become a tenured professor. This whole process will take several decades if it happens at all. There is a lot of competition, and not that many spaces are available. Much like business…

I'll admit that the PhD is the most sure-fire way of becoming an academic. However, the question you really have to ask yourself is as follows: "what does being an academic mean to you?" Because if it means working for a university, there are different pathways. If it means doing research, see point 2. If it means doing teaching, there are again, many other pathways of reaching that goal. Make sure you don't stare yourself blind on the idea of a PhD, simply because you forgot to consider any alternatives.

2. You want to continue working in research

Again, I don't think a PhD is the only way to continue working in research. As I mentioned before, being a business collaborator means you'd work in business (often earns more, just saying) but would continue working with academics on projects. It often means that there are more projects, a different working pace and a very different earning potential. A VERY different earning potential.

To be honest, the potential of working yourself up also seems to be higher. Business has a higher progression rate than academia. Whereas in 3 to 7 years you go from first-year PhD student to Dr, a lot of my friends will have held two or three different job titles in that time, and that's simply because they're rising through the ranks, not assuming they only hold jobs for 1 year and then move on to the next one.

Additionally, the days that research was exclusively associated with academia are well behind us. And with well behind us I mean at least 50 years behind us. There are plenty of research-focused companies, units, agencies, consultancies and government subdivisions that have nothing to do with academia, yet produce great and even publishable research. Be open-minded and realistic as to what your goal is. If it's research, a PhD really is not an obligation by any means.

One sidenote here as well. If you are very certain about your field and topic of interest, and after careful market research you do find that for the types of jobs that you see yourself doing require a PhD, well that's me out of ammo. I'm just trying to emphasize that this need not be the case and that sometimes work experience in research is much more valuable than the research experience gained from doing a PhD. So, make sure you're basing this choice on actual facts with regard to the market you're wanting to work in rather than your misconceptions of that market. Just saying.

3. A PhD will give you a large advantage in the job market

Having mentioned the job market, do your research! As I said earlier, sometimes a PhD will give you an advantage, sometimes it's a prerequisite and sometimes it's just an idea you have about the job market that's absolutely baseless.

If you want to be an academic for sure, and then I mean the type of academic who does a PhD, post-doc, assistant professorship, yada yada yada... yes, the PhD will have advantages in the job market. Quite frankly, you won't have too much of a choice in doing a PhD; it's the "easiest" way in.

A PhD also represents the research you have done, gives you time to publish that research (sometimes) and as such gives you value as a job applicant to academic positions. Not to mention that the network of academics is likely to know you. But are you sure it will give you the same advantage in any other sector?

Moving from academia into industry is becoming an increasingly popular move, but it remains a "controversial" one in the eyes of those who've never left academia and did their PhDs when dinosaurs were still around. The reason for this is partially due to the commercialization of education, which I promise I will explain eventually.

Looking at industry, I think you need to be really sure that the advantage of doing a PhD is as big as you think it is, before investing 3 to 7 years into academic research rather than work experience. Because 3 to 7 years of work experience is of immense value as well.

In addition to the value of work experience, we need to come back to the concept of opportunity costs. Are you sure that 3 to 7 years of doing a PhD is going to improve your advantage in the job market, predominantly the non-academic job market, much more than any other possible action? Is there a better way of directing your resources? Keep in mind, work experience is also important. And often, a PhD doesn't count as work experience.

4. You have a keen interest in studying a specific topic/project

Let's say you want to do a PhD because of a genuine interest. First of all, congrats on finding something you truly find interesting, that can take people years, if not decades to figure out. Second, are you sure you find this topic really THAT interesting to commit 3 to 7 years to it? Third, are you willing to deviate from that topic or the method of which you would study it in? Because that is what often tends to happen in a PhD. It's your PhD, but you're working within a team of supervisors and collaborators. If they aren't feeling it, it's likely not going to happen. And then what? If that would wipe out your entire motivation for the project, I don't think applying to a PhD is in your best interest, because I think you'd drop out just as quickly.

This doesn't apply to all PhDs in the same way. There are PhD projects that are entirely shaped beforehand, for which the potential PhD applicant simply applies. They then join a much bigger project, often with several PhD students working on adjacent topics or projects. You see this often in the hard sciences, such as neuroscience, biology, physics, etc. The potential switching of methodologies and non-set structures beforehand applies more to the formative type of PhD programs often seen in the social sciences and humanities, where both parties talk through the topic, design and implementation in the first year and shape the PhD together. Fields in which this is more common are business, economics, psychology, etc. I'm raising this point to flag up that you have to be very committed to a topic, yet quite flexible with regard to its execution, if this is your main motivation for doing a PhD.

Also, as I mentioned in point 2, research can happen in many places that aren't academia. So, first figure out whether academia is even the best fit, with regard to both the structure and the approach to studying your topic of interest. Otherwise, revisit point 2 and find yourself another research institute that does a lot of work in the area you are interested in.

The Practicalities of Doing a PhD

We've now discussed terrible reasons for doing a PhD and we've critically evaluated seemingly good reasons for doing a PhD. If by this stage you're still 100% onboard with doing a PhD, then let's dive into the practicalities of doing the PhD or just the 5W's and the 1H: what, why, where, who, when and how.

What?

What are you going to do in your PhD? Which topics are you studying? To what extent would you like to study one specific topic? These are questions to ask. For example, if you have a master's degree in economics, going into an economics, finance or business PhD makes a lot of sense, if you really want to do a PhD.

But within each of these fields, there is a vast range of topics. Even if you "just" want to do behavioral science, which is the field my PhD was in, what part of it? Do you like biases or would you rather build a prescriptive model of decision-making in stock investments? I don't mean to scare you. It would just be a good start to pinpoint a topic. Preferably a really specific one. You don't need an exact research question yet, but it would help. A lot.

It will help as you will need to apply to a PhD with a research proposal, outlining what you want to study and how. The better you can explain this, the higher your chances of being accepted.

On the topic of how, as a subset of the "what", defining your research topic also includes its methodology. How do you want to approach your topic of interest? Certain institutions and people specialize in certain methods, so this will partially guide your search for the right fit of program for you.

Additionally, there is a more overarching question that falls into the remit of *what*: what do you want from your PhD? This refers back to the previous chapter as well, where it determines whether a PhD is the only way or even the best way to get to your overarching goal.

Why?

Ask yourself why. Why do you want to do a PhD? Don't take doing a PhD lightly. Even my most passionate peers are banging their heads against the wall from time to time.

However, this is not the main "why" that's of interest here. I'm not really asking you why you want to do a PhD. By this stage of the book, you should've figured out why you want to do a PhD and whether that reason is good enough to keep you going. I outline several bad reasons and several good reasons that you still need to remain critical of in the previous chapters. The why in this chapter is as follows: why do you want to study your topic of interest?

This is a question for both yourself and the several statements you'll need to write for your PhD applications (more on the application process in the next chapter). You will need to convincingly communicate your interest in this topic. If you are really struggling coming up with reasons for why you want to do a PhD *in a specific topic*, it might be that the topic is not for you. Or even, that the PhD as a whole is not for you.

Where?

Once you have established a topic and a motivation for that topic, the next question is where?

Where is a question with many considerations. If you don't have to take any limitations into account, where is probably the institution that has the highest ranking when it comes to your topic or has the world's foremost researcher in that topic in employment.

However, most people do have to take limitations into consideration: where can you go financially? Where can you go without entry and resident restrictions, if those pose an issue to you? Where can your family go or where are they willing to go, granted that you have a family who's coming with you? Suddenly, the world is no longer your oyster and these are serious considerations to take into account.

So, with these restrictions in place, where can you go? The general approach remains the same: most people are chasing down a certain level of status within a degree. Having a PhD from a top-ranked university is definitely advantageous. As a result, having determined your topic and your geo-location of comfort, select which university ranks highest in your topic and start looking for a supervisor there.

This is tricky as you might not know these people at all. Staying at the university where you studied your master's tends to be easier, as you know the location and the people. Supervisors tend to prefer hiring people they already know and have taught, compared to those who they have never met. But just because it is easier, doesn't mean it is better.

Another *where* that we should look at loops in nicely with how we ended the *what*: where do you want to end up after your PhD? This is more important than people think. If you want your academic career to be based in the US, doing a non-US PhD is not that smart. It makes getting more difficult (not impossible, just more difficult). The reason for this is the difference in PhD program duration. As mentioned before, in the UK, PhD programs are notably shorter (3 to 4 years) than in the US (5 to 7 years). This difference matters, so take it into account.

Having established the "where", let's look at the "who"!

Who?

The institution isn't the only one that determines the value of your degree. Ranking can also come in terms of people. In your PhD program, you'll have at least one supervisor, who has of course specialized in their own topic and does research in this topic. This is why I indicated that you need to know *what* you'd like to study because this will determine in what field and topic you'll look for a supervisor. Your supervisor needs to match your topic to a certain extent, but they need to match your methodology and your personality even more.

If both you and your preliminary supervisor study contactless payment methods, that is great (that was my initial PhD topic). But it's going to be an issue if you want to study this using qualitative interviews and individual case studies, whereas your supervisor is a quantitative data scientist. This won't work. Your supervisor in this case can't help you with your methodology at all. And if they can't help you with a rather important aspect of your PhD research, that's not such a good fit. So make sure you look for supervisors in both your topic and your preferred methodology.

A quick sidenote here: this advice is much more important for shorter PhD programs without training, in which it is assumed that you have certain skills (experimental design and data analysis). However, if your PhD has internal training, as often seen in the US, this means that you have 2 years to train yourself in a certain methodology, to fit the expertise of your preliminary supervisor. If that is the case, this aspect of *who* doesn't matter as much, if at all.

Moving from topic and methodology to personality and work ethic. What kind of person are you and how do you work? If you're laid-back and can easily work on your own, you won't need hands-on supervision as much. So, it's not the end of the world if your potential supervisor already has quite a few PhD students and post-docs. But if you're like me and prefer to have weekly meetings with your supervisor(s) (I had two), having a laid-back, thin-spread supervisor will only backfire. Keep in mind, you are going to spend hours upon hours with these people. This is a long commitment. Choose wisely.

Now, I mentioned this in the *where* section as well, but it's tricky if you don't know these people at all. There are quite a few people who select the location of their master's degree as a way to get to know their teachers better and vet them as possible supervisors. It sounds quite hardcore, but it's really a good strategy, if you can look that far ahead!

Don't worry, there's a more in-depth chapter on selecting the right supervisor for you.

When?

Also, a question to keep in mind: when are you going to do this? The main question is whether you want to do this now or later in life. Work experience first and then back into academia? Many of my peers have followed this trajectory. They say it has definitely been a process of getting back into a "student mentality". On the other hand, they have valuable work experience, which many of my friends and I don't have. We're still in the student mentality because we've never been anything else.

There are arguments to be made for both. If you stay in education and do a PhD straight after your master's degree, you'll know more people that can hire you as a PhD student, and they know you as well (assuming you remain in the same institution). This does increase your chances of being hired.

However, having work experience beforehand can also definitely be an advantage. People who move from industry back into academia via a PhD tend to be much more resilient and independent. They seem to be much better prepared for what's going on and prospective supervisors and institutions do perceive them as such. This of course is traded off against the fact that transitioning back will require a lot more networking to actually get there.

A second question to ask with regard to timing is as follows: full-time or part-time? Having mentioned finances before, not everyone can take out 3 to 7 years from their (financial) lives to do a PhD. In agreement with your employer, you might be able to do a PhD part-time. As a result, the process of the PhD will be longer, but less intense. It can then be combined with a job, so the decrease in income is not as severe.

It might not even be in regard to just finance. Some of my colleagues have jobs *and* families. Quitting the job is not an option as it supports the family. The solution is doing a part-time PhD. But trust me, juggling those three things is real hard work. And you might consider doing the PhD later in life, when both your career is more stable and your family is older.

How?

Last but not least, maybe almost most importantly: how are you going to do your PhD? This question can be interpreted in many ways as well. If we take it quite narrowly, it can mean what methodology would you like to use? As I outlined before, this is important for your application. The more detail you can use, the better. It might make your application stand out even more if the methodology you use is quite innovative in itself or if you wish to propose a whole new methodology altogether. The latter of course also comes with a certain risk and it is nowhere near necessary to go this crazy for a PhD application. Just make sure you know what you want to do and how you'd like to do it. What are you already able to do and what are you willing to learn?

On a broader scale, it can mean: how are you going to do a PhD *financially*? Especially when leaving a job to go into a PhD, you will lose income. There is a flipside to coming from a job: some employers fund PhDs for their employees, if they study something that benefits the company. I personally think this is a great opportunity. It adds to the *why* as well: a great opportunity to benefit all.

Luckily, PhDs can be funded without having had a job before. But this tends to be another application process in itself. Often, there are grants given by the institutions themselves, some governmental ones for excellency or social applicability and lastly scholarships for foreign students specifically, such as Chancellors in the UK.

Ultimately, not everyone gets funded. Ask yourself then: can I make it without funding? Can I accept those kinds of living conditions and am I willing to? Without inserting too much of my opinion here, I personally believe doing a PhD without funding is a form of exploitation and would never recommend it.

The Uno reverse card

Now, I did write this chapter in a certain order: what, why, where, who, when and how. But no one said this was the only order in which to approach those questions!

I've heard of some cases where people would only apply to a single institution, regardless of the supervisor or even the specific topic and methodology. If you think that's niche: there are also people who consider doing a PhD but only with one specific supervisor. Keep in mind though, if there's a person you really want to work with, do not be surprised if you have to adjust your topic and methodology to their expertise. To take this completely out of proportion: you wouldn't go to Daniel Kahneman (Nobel Prize Winner in Economics) to study Higgs boson.

As I said, I don't know many people who approach doing a PhD this way, but it can be done. This does require a lot more work at the start, such as networking. Because non-conforming PhD application routes work better when the potential PhD student already knows their prospective supervisor(s) before the PhD is started.

The how can also lead to the who: if you are in need of funding, seek out a supervisor who has recently received a massive grant. This might also change the topic and methodology of your PhD. Grants are often given on the basis of a research proposal, so topic, methodology, resources and time period are locked in. If you can live with that, go for it!

If by any means you're aware of more of these combinations and order reversals, let me know!

Biggest Misconceptions of Doing a PhD

Now that we have established bad and good reasons for doing a PhD, let's do some expectation management so you know what you're in for. I asked my PhD colleagues what the 10 biggest misconceptions they had about doing a PhD were. I thought I'd outline them for you here.

1. Everyone around you is smarter or better at research

I can promise you, this is not true. Most people put on a good show or a brave face, but everyone is struggling with some aspect, if not a lot of aspects of their PhD. The issue here is that you're comparing your entire developmental process to their finished and polished end result.

This process of social comparison leads to what is known as the imposter syndrome: because you're comparing your struggle to someone else's success (upward social comparison), you're going to feel as if you don't deserve to be there at all. That you getting into the PhD program was somehow a mistake and that you're going to be found out any moment now. I've been waiting all of my PhD for this; it never happened.

As you get to know your colleagues and their work better and you get together and honestly talk through what you and your work are going through as a sort of therapy session, you'll figure out they're in a mess just as big as yours. Maybe even bigger.

PhD projects (well, academic research in general) are notoriously messy. Five things have to backfire before anything works. Code stops running, hypotheses were fundamentally flawed, the initial method isn't measuring what it's supposed to or you cannot get access to the sample you need. These issues will happen to you and you'll feel worse for it. Until you talk to someone else and they are going through the same (or a similar) thing. There's no pain like shared pain.

2. You have a clearly defined role

No one seems to know what a PhD student really is. At least, most of the time our departments can't figure it out. You're invited to some staff meetings but not to others. Some things are mandatory, others you can be exempt from as a "student". Yes, you will teach but on an hourly rate. And you're still being paid a terribly low wage (if you're on a scholarship).

There'll always be a distance between the actual staff and the PhD students. Sometimes, it's just more noticeable than others. So, you're not really a student, but you're not a member of staff either. Just hanging in the void between the two. It's odd, I know. It's unsurprising that there's a lot of ongoing debate on whether a PhD is a job or not. I think it is, others think it isn't. Just prepare yourself for a lack of a clear definition of what you are.

3. Your supervisor is in charge of the project and is in control

A friend of mine thought it would be a 50/50 division between themselves and their supervisor on how to design, plan and implement the research. Not so much. It was more like 85% theirs, and their supervisor would check the other 15% every so often to make sure they were still somewhat on the same page.

Now with this control do come some benefits. It is YOUR project. So, if the way your supervisor(s) handle the work and you as a person isn't working for you, you can and should indicate this and create a workflow that does work. I know PhD students who actually gave some of this control away, to make sure they progressed at a decent speed, by meeting deadlines as imposed by their supervisor(s). Whatever works. We have this control, as such, we should use it.

I do want to put a disclaimer on this: the control division depends on the field, department, university and supervisor you're with. If you're in a massive structure PhD (more often seen in the hard sciences), with strict deadlines, a predetermined methodology, etc., your control is obviously a lot less. The experience outlined above was from a friend at the Warwick Business School, who was in an unstructured PhD project (a.k.a. "build your own").

4. The project you applied with will be the project for your PhD

This one might seem a bit counterintuitive, but it's not necessarily true. The disclaimer from earlier continues to apply: it depends on how structured the PhD program you applied to is.

For unstructured or just less structured PhD programs, the general idea still holds that once you signed up for something, you're stuck with that something. But this doesn't seem to be true. There are two different scenarios here that I'd like to share.

I applied to doing a PhD with the idea of running a longitudinal study on nudging people's saving behavior. That was my research proposal. I ended up writing up five short-term chapters on how different payment methods affect people's ability to manage their finances. No, that's not remotely the same thing. This happened to one of my closest friends at another university as well. Their PhD application included a research proposal on promoting voting behavior. They are currently studying ways to improve medication adherence. It happens.

Our research topics changed quite naturally. For them, it was a grant that their supervisor received for medication adherence, so she got onboarded onto that topic. For me, it was the popularization of contactless payment methods in the UK that shifted my focus. But the change of topic can be a lot less natural and gradual: your project could just not work.

If the research isn't working, as in, if the topic no longer works for you, or the method doesn't, or the results just weren't as great as you hoped, you can drop it and move on. It's actually recommended that you do. In the same way that it is recommended to run several projects at the same time.

Now, I'm not saying this is an easy process. Sometimes a different method just means running a study differently, that's fine, it just means more work. But other times, it means having to find a different supervisor or even department, if your topic or method switch is quite extreme. Don't beat yourself up about it, this does happen!

5. You'll just be doing research, nothing else

Afraid not, you'll have quite a few other obligations in the PhD program. Research is simply one of many tasks of the job.

With most PhD programs, there'll be several hoops you'll have to jump through before getting started. Some of these hoops will be mandatory courses. So suddenly you find yourself back in a lecture hall and not as the lecturer. This easily knocks 1 or 2 years of the PhD (depends on the program).

From there onwards, you're not done either. The PhD is your project, so it's your administrative responsibility. And there is a surprisingly large amount of admin that needs to happen when doing research. Administrative things to take into account: pre-registration, funding/grant applications, ethics applications (that is a process…), participant recruitment and selection, and that is just for one project. And then there might be some other miscellaneous stuff: in my first year of the PhD, I had to hand in another dissertation due to my funding scheme. That is a lot of hours I'm not going to get back to do my actual research. But then again, who cares?

Next to admin, another job which will take quite a lot of time is teaching. A lot of people do really enjoy teaching and sign up to it voluntarily. Others need the additional money teaching brings in. Some are stuck in contracts that mandate they need to teach a certain amount of hours to "earn" their stipend (you really need to watch out for these contracts…). Whatever your reason for teaching may be, it costs time. Time not spent on research. You get what I am saying?

6. There will be a lot of collaboration on projects within your research group

One of my colleagues is still disappointed by the lack of collaboration they have seen when it comes to people helping each other out in their projects. Academia is known for being filled with collaborations, where multiple people get together, think about a cool topic, work out the pragmatics and do cool research together. But this is not at all how the PhD seems to work.

The PhD seems to be much more individual. Sure, you can get together and talk about your topic and any issues you might be having and I'm sure colleagues will chip in with some feedback and maybe help you out a bit, but that's it. It'll still be your project. During the PhD, it is highly unlikely there will be a project that isn't yours, but "ours".

Now, I do have to mention what I suspect drives this "individualism". There are regulations as to what can be put in the final PhD thesis and the emphasis is on it being the work of an individual. Collaborations, proper collaborations, have quite harsh requirements to qualify for this. As such, it is not that surprising that on the PhD level, with a clear deadline ahead, the focus on collaborations is minimal.

7. A PhD will end up being similar to a 9–5 job, working 40 hours a week

There seems to be no end to this one: a PhD is not a 9–5 if you don't want it to be! If you want to work like hell for 1 month and not do anything the next, you can. Up to you (unless your supervisors have strong reservations). Is that recommendable? Not sure, but if it works for you, go for it. You don't even have to work from the office, if you prefer working from home, or from the Bahamas!

Some restrictions there: if you work in a lab, you might need to be in that lab. Unless that lab is in the Bahamas, the previous statement might be rather difficult to fulfill. Just putting that out there, I don't want to get your hopes up.

Now, I will mention something that I think is key: flexibility can massively backfire. No one will send you home at 17:00. If you want to keep working until 21:00, you can. But the real question is whether you should. Don't overwork yourself because you think that is what everyone else is doing. The flexibility in work schedules makes it difficult to judge how long everyone else is working.

In general, how long someone is working is by no means a sign of their productivity. I can do admin for 10 hours. It's depressing, but I can as it doesn't require much mental capacity. I can code for 8 hours (just refuse to do so for my own sanity). I can write for 6 at best. So, to me a 10-hour working day might have been less productive than a 6-hour one. Because in the former I just did admin, whereas in the latter, I will have written thousands of words. That's quite a difference.

Additionally, not everyone works at the same pace or has the same attention span. Don't compare yourself to others, don't compare your working routine to that of others, and design a routine that works for you, and makes you produce high-quality work, within the remit of certain deadlines and expectations. If this means working 9–5, 5 days a week, 40 hours long, that's fine. If it doesn't mean that, also fine. Just get it done.

8. In a PhD, you will have to promote yourself less

If you wanted to escape the shameless self-promotion by avoiding taking a job in business, I've got some terrible news for you.

Academia is competitive too. It is possible (read: likely) that you aren't exactly the only researcher in your topic, although it can feel that way sometimes. So, you need to be able to sell yourself to get access to unique research opportunities. I'm referring to how you define yourself in your department, your research group, but also at conferences and other networking events. You'll have to sell your own capabilities as well as the validity of your own research. You need to believe that you are the best person to do this, having employed the best methods of obtaining the most interesting results ever. Yes I know, not my cup of tea either. But self-deprecation (my sense of humor) tends to come across as insecurity and not believing in your own research. And if the researcher doesn't even believe in it, why should the audience even care?

9. Your project is awesome and people care about it as much as you do

Would you care as much about other people's projects as your own? Exactly. You care about your project, naturally (hopefully). You think it's pretty awesome (I hope). Otherwise, see the previous point and pretend you think it's extremely awesome. But the issue is, you are the only one that cares THIS much. Which is exactly why you need to sell your research to begin with.

If something goes wrong within your research, people will sympathize, but they won't actually care. Because it is not their project. This might even hold for your supervisors. They will have many more than one PhD student (you), so they run into problems with their supervisees' research all the time. They will run into issues with their very own research as well. This project might be your whole world, but it isn't theirs (nor should it be). So that can cause some initial frictions. Good advice I've been given? Find yourself a group of people who do similar stuff or have an interest that is similar to yours and your project. You can nerd out together. It'll be good for you!

10. You won't get that much feedback as it's YOUR project

Counterintuitively, although you are the one who cares the most, your own feedback is not the one that matters most. Nor the one that you'll think about most. If you hand in written work, your supervisors will ply you with feedback. I think for the first paper I wrote, which is a short paper btw, I got over 60 comments for every page, for every draft. There were quite a few drafts… In a sense, this is great though because my supervisors do put in the work!

But that's not all. Your presented work will get plenty of feedback too. During conferences, or even informal talks, there'll be questions, suggestions or just plain criticisms of what you are doing. Some of this feedback will be very useful, actual constructive criticism will be given to you. But there'll also be feedback that is just utterly useless, telling you that your project sucks or whatever. So, expect the worst, but keep in mind that this type of feedback reflects more on whoever says it rather than on you or your project.

Well, I think 10 misconceptions are more than enough to start us off with. Keep in mind that it is important to have the right expectations when starting a PhD, so as to not be caught too off-guard or just be plain disappointed and disillusioned. The best way of avoiding this is to talk to people currently in PhD programs. Ask them about their experiences in the PhD program, working with specific people (particularly supervisors) or being at specific institutions. Gather as much information as you can before making the decision to do a PhD. I can promise it'll only help!

So Should You Do a PhD?

We started off with terrible reasons to do a PhD, then critically evaluated good reasons to do a PhD, moved onto the practicalities of doing a PhD and last we debunked some misconceptions with those who know better. We have come full circle: should you do a PhD?

I can imagine that the setup of this section might not have been exactly what you expected. But I included this for a reason: you shouldn't think of doing a PhD lightly. You need to have a strong motivation for doing the PhD (Chapter 2), need to know what you're getting into (Chapter 4) and need a very good plan about how and what you're going to do (Chapter 3). The reason I keep hammering on this is quite simple: there are rather adverse consequences if you don't. To underestimate the PhD is to bargain for lots of stress and possible mental health issues. I've seen this before. I've experienced this myself.

Truth time: I entered the PhD straight from my master's degree. I was 20 years old when I moved to the UK (from the Netherlands). I was excited about doing my master's degree, my first experience living abroad and my next step for preparing my career in behavioral science. The master's was great! But one curious thing with Warwick University is that at the same time you start your degree, they start running career fairs. No joke, this was almost immediate. I went to the fairs, figured out all my possible options (somehow only looking at consultancies?) and went through the motions. I did the applications, the written statements, the training centers and after all that, the interviews. I went down to London, excited, wet behind the ears, and just did it. And hated all of it.

By this stage, it's late November, about 8 weeks after the master's started. I'm disappointed but also in distress about not knowing what to do after my master's. I told this to one of my teachers. He's teaching us statistical analysis in R. It's not exactly my best course… We plan a meeting to discuss it further, and we do so about a week later. He asks me about my interests, I tell him that my main interests are looking into the motivations behind spending and saving behavior and he recommends I look into doing a PhD. A week later, after having done the bare minimum of research, I tell him that I'm going to apply to PhD programs and will apply to Warwick as well. He then agrees to be my supervisor for the PhD program at Warwick and actually helps me craft my research proposal as well, which is then sent to a multitude of different universities. I do receive several offers, but my heart is set on Warwick, and by January, I know I've been accepted into the program with full funding.

Now, this might not exactly sound like a horror story, and it isn't. But the amount of possible pitfalls in that story just glare at me. There are so many turns and twists that this could've gone wrong at and have gone wrong for some of my friends and have gone wrong for others I don't even know. And this section was to make you aware of those possible pitfalls and to make sure that you do prepare.

As I said in the introduction of this book: worst-case scenario, I'll tell you about my mistakes, so you can recognize and avoid them.

If your motivation for doing a PhD remains unchanged, let's dive into the practicalities of actually applying to the sucker!

Section 2

Applying to the PhD

Okay, so we've now figured out that you're definitely going to apply to a PhD. Cool. But how do you go about that?

In the previous chapters, I outlined the need for knowing a few practicalities before even deciding that you're actually doing a PhD. It's important to know, before even thinking of applying, which topics you're interested in, which universities you're interested in and to have a rough idea of which people you'd be interested in working with. But those were rather vague ideas. Now, it's time to make them rather concrete.

There are several ways of applying to a PhD. You can do it the "cold" way and the "hot" way. The former is also known as cold calling, which is why I've made the distinction in the way that I did.

A cold application is going through the university's PhD application system, without having a preconceived idea of who your supervisor would be. When asked the question whether you are applying with a supervisor, the answer is "no". In this type of application, what will happen is that your submitted documents will be reviewed and if found to be satisfactory, they will be laid in front of the research group or department you're applying to, and their academics will decide whether they'd fancy taking you on as a PhD student. If no one likes your topic, your methodology, or your application in general, you don't get chosen. Despite your application being satisfactory qualitywise, you still receive a rejection.

A hot application is the opposite. You'll go through the university's PhD application process having talked to your potential supervisor(s) before. You can select their name when applying, and if you've been really lucky, they'll even have helped you with some aspects of the application process, such as the research proposal or the funding. Having their name on things from the start ensures a higher success rate. Having them review your documents and even suggest edits ensures they are of higher quality. This method has a much higher success rate as a result. If your submitted documents have been reviewed and found to be satisfactory, your potential supervisor will "claim" you and you will receive an offer. Often, this offer is conditional on you satisfying several other criteria, such as a financial check and the completion of education.

From the get-go, I want to have this difference established. I'd like to mention that the success rate for a "hot" application is much higher and is also my preferred method. However, I will describe both these approaches in the chapters in this section. So, let's dive in.

Finding a Topic

Although your main field of interest and topics of interest were already established in the previous section, this now needs to be narrowed down even further. What *exactly* do you want to study? This means research question(s), hypotheses, methodology, timeline, expected resources to be used, etc.

To find a topic you're really going to have to dig deep. This type of "soul-searching" often gets accompanied with a lot of introspection and talking to friends, family and colleagues. What do you care deeply about? Why do you care about it? Has there been a lot of work in this field already, or not? Is there a specific question no one has asked yet? Or in economic speak: is there a gap in the market? Would you be interested in filling that gap? If so, how?

Obviously, knowing whether there is a gap in the market requires less introspection and more actual research. You're going to need to read up on your topic(s) of interest. To make this more concrete, let's consider an example.

You're really interested in financial decision-making. Moreover, within that subfield of decision-making, your main interest is looking into why people aren't saving. Even more specific, you want to know why people aren't saving for unforeseen expenses, also known as the rainy-day fund (I'm in this subfield of study, that's why I know). There is literature on this already. There is an entire field of literature dedicated to decision-making and financial decision-making within it. A large chunk of that literature does revolve around saving behavior. And within that subcategory of financial decision-making, there is a further split into the different types of things people save for: short-term goals, long-term goals, education, retirement, children, investing and the rainy-day fund (this is a non-exhaustive list). You've now identified the general literature on saving behavior and several subcategories within that literature.

Don't be scared of the time commitment here: A large chunk of this will result in the main skeleton and even some of the flesh of the research proposal and your research motivation (this can be its own document or part of the personal statement). But I admit even then, this is a hefty commitment. But then again, if you don't want to even commit this much time and effort, the PhD might not be for you. If you cannot commit this much time, the PhD is also very likely not going to be for you, but there are many more factors to consider if that is the case, and I don't want to slight you by combining you with the previous group of people.

Anyway, back to the topic at hand: your topic. Your topic will come to you via a deep dive into the literature that you already find interesting. You'll go through more and more work and see what has already been done, what has been found, what methods have been applied, and potentially what the current limitations are and ideas for further research. Also, I should clarify this, when I refer to literature, I mean academic literature. So, the types of research papers that are published in peer-reviewed journals can be accessed via search engines, such as Google Scholar.

In addition to this, you'll also get even more exposure to what type of work is publishable. And this is quite important in a PhD. Published papers like this (with an emphasis on more recently published papers) will tell you what level of quality is expected. Don't worry, your research proposal need not resemble this level yet!

All in all, do a lot of research. Read a lot of papers. If you feel like you're grasping what's going on in the literature, start summarizing it, preferably in a somewhat systematic way. Who has done what? Which sources are they referencing to support their hypotheses? What did they find? How did they find it? What were the limitations of that work? How have others contributed to it? Are there still gaps in knowledge? What work still needs to be done to further our understanding of what's going on? How could you contribute to this?

The long list of questions I've just outlined is almost literally the structure of your research proposal. Just saying.

So, this is my main strategy for finding yourself a topic. But at the same time that you're doing this, given that you've found yourself a subfield (from the example: financial decision-making), you can, and probably should, look at universities and people that rank high in this (sub)field. So let's look at that now!

Finding a University

Once you've found yourself a topic, or even just a subfield or field of interest, it's time to determine where to take it. Looking back at the previous section: *where* do you want to do your PhD?

In Chapter 3, we already discussed that there might be limitations as to where you're going. You might not be able to move to the other side of the world, and that's completely fine, no one said you had to.

If you can't leave the city or area you're currently living in, your options are so restricted that this chapter can essentially be skipped. If there are multiple universities in your city/area, make sure to check their ranking in your (sub)field of choice, and go from there. Once we're talking country or continent level, we need a slightly more systematic approach. And if the world is in fact your oyster, and there are no restrictions, things ironically become a lot more complicated.

Luckily, people have identified this issue ages ago. If you google your topic or (sub)field of interest, there'll be several university rankings, telling you which university or even department ranks the highest. You can easily adapt these rankings to only reflect certain parts of the world, such as your country of residence, or a continent of choice. Pro-tip: do check what these rankings are based on. If there's a lot of weight placed on factors you don't actually care about, move onto a different ranking system. Trust me, there are loads.

If you still don't like any of the ranking systems after having gone through all of them, call a friend. Well, in this case, they're more likely to be a stranger and you will email rather than call them, but the principle stands. Universities often have a list of their current PhD students on their website. This means you will find their name, topic of study and email quite quickly. PhD students are quite used to people reaching out to them to discuss the PhD (I mean, I'm really used to it, but that might just be because of the blog). Nothing is easier than setting up a 20-minute online meeting to answer some of your questions about their experience. It's only 20 minutes of their life and it might help you out loads. Most PhD students won't refuse you the time, trust me.

Another thing I've also mentioned is that the university you choose for your PhD will have an impact on where you go next. The most notable impact is that it's very difficult to take a non-US PhD degree to the US. If you've been dreaming about going to the US for decades, it's probably advisable to do your PhD there, granted that you can afford it. If you cannot, make sure to look into collaborative networks. Which US-based universities are working with universities that you would be able to afford?

I'm going to be honest; this will require some FBI-level type of research. This is not information which is super easy to find if you don't know where to look.

So, that's my advice for finding yourself a good university for your PhD: establish your restrictions and preferred area of study, rank all the universities that fall within this area, reach out to people already doing a PhD at your preferred universities and take it from there.

Now that you've got the basics down for finding a university, let's look at some people!

Finding a Supervisor

You can easily read this chapter before the previous one, the order of these isn't as set as you might think. Just a heads up! But if we're approaching these chapters in chronological order (and you really don't have to), what you now need to do is to look at the specific research groups that focus on your topic, or adjacent topics, at the universities that you have selected. Find out whether they host academics who study your specific topic or your specific subfield.

From the rainy-day fund example that I keep using: find out in each university whether they have a behavioral science, economics, psychology or marketing group that has people in it that study saving behavior or maybe even go as broad as looking at financial decision-making. If they even have someone studying rainy-day fund savings, you're golden. But it's definitely not necessary to find yourself a Cinderella fit.

You might have also just noticed that I quoted four different types of research groups for one topic. Financial decision-making has a rather wide remit: it garners interest from economists, psychologists, behavioral scientists and marketeers. One way of finding this out is to look at the journals' research on financial decision-making gets published in. Look at their titles and the subject they tend to often be associated with. This can guide your search with specific research groups and departments from the start, making sure you don't exclusively focus on one subject, completely ignoring another subject which could still be a good fit for you. This does tend to happen much more with interdisciplinary fields, however.

Having discussed the chapters in chronological order, there is obviously another way of finding a supervisor. Which is the reverse.

Starting once more from your topic or (sub)field: who are the most prominent people doing research there? I have to admit, this process is 10 times easier if you're dealing with a specific topic (e.g. rainy-day fund savings) rather than a subfield (savings) or an entire field (financial decision-making).

Let's assume you've done lots of reading on your topic already. And when I say "let's assume", I mean that it would be strongly recommended you have in fact already done this. In addition to topical knowledge and publication standards, this will also have given you an idea of who's working in this field. Their names are on the papers after all.

This then becomes a strong indicator of who to aim for. Next question is then: where are they based? If they are based in a location you have pre-selected in the previous chapter, great, add them to the list. If not, drop them. Don't keep them in the back of your head or on a different list. If you can't afford going to the location where they're based, don't torture yourself with "what might have been".

Now, we have a list of people and research groups. Despite having aimed for people before looking at locations, it would still be smart to check out other academics in the research group your preferred person is based at. This just widens the net and gives you a second and maybe even several other ranked choices, if your first choice will not take you on as their PhD student.

Whichever chronological order you choose to do this process in, you're going to end up with a list of people at places you can go. The trick now is to reach out to these people and convince them to hire you. Preferably, even get to know them. Easy peasy. Right?

Reaching out to a person is very easy these days. A lot of their details should be easily found via their university page, as well as their social media. I would suggest going through their university pages first, before using social media. The latter is really more of a last resort, unless you know them really well. When sending potential supervisors an email, it helps if you have a certain set of key points: who you are, what you do and how this is relevant to them. Don't take three paragraphs to get to the latter point. Most academics get a lot of emails and are barely skimming most of them. It needs to be short but clear as to what you want from them. That's all that's really required when it comes to reaching out to them.

More difficult is to convince them to actually take you on or even help you with the application. I will admit that people who actively know their potential supervisor (e.g. they've been taught by them in undergraduate or master's) have a great advantage here. So, before you even apply to doing a PhD, network your sweet heart out or even direct your previous degrees targeting the university or person you want to work with. If you're not in this massively advantageous position, let's at least try to level up your application from a cold one to a lukewarm one!

To get someone to hire you, without really knowing you, you need to make sure they seemingly get to know you. As mentioned earlier, your email needs to be short but clear, and preferably would also include a draft of a research proposal enclosed. Yes, you will need to have written a version of this already to be taken seriously. Your email and your proposal also need to be tailored to the specific person and university (or department or research group) you're applying to. If it's clearly a "copy + paste" email, you're not exactly scoring points. Don't panic: the general structure and topic of your research proposal and e-mail will largely remain the same, and I do recommend writing down a "base" version of both of these, before creating tailored versions for specific people and universities.

So you've written up some documents that hopefully multiple people have proofread for you and you've sent them out to your people of choice, now what? Well, now we wait. There is the general stereotype that academics aren't good with email because they're hardly tethered to this earthly plane anyway, but that's a load of crock. Some people will get back to you instantly, some you will have to email at least five times. The latter seems to scare people off, but with PhD application deadlines looming, can you afford to be this passive? My rule of thumb: if you don't have a reply within a week, resend the email.

Eventually, replies will, slowly, come trickling in. Some will be immediate rejections, others will be really vague non-committal replies (after two such emails, cut your losses) and some will be interested in progressing things. In the first case, do ask why they rejected you. Chances of getting an email back aren't super high, but it's likely to be a useful form of feedback. In the second case, there's not much to do. In both these two cases, you now reach out to your second choice of person at that department or research group, if you've identified a second choice there. Otherwise, drop that group as an option. In the third case, where there is a possibility of acceptance, continue to communicate.

Communication with a potentially interested supervisor is a careful balancing act. You need to balance your relief and eagerness with caution and realism. You need to get to know them to see if they're actually a good fit. If you're lucky, they'll set up an online call with you, where you can talk things through. This doesn't always happen; some of these people are incredibly busy. Whether the online call does or doesn't happen is actually a pretty good indicator of how much time they'll make for you once you're being supervised by them.

If you still want to know more about your potential supervisor but can't get to know them directly, get to know them indirectly. In the previous chapter, I've already mentioned that current PhD students are a great resource when it comes to painting you a realistic picture of a university or department. Well, they're even better at dishing out info on their respective supervisors. I don't mean this in a nasty gossipy way (I mean, it's possible I suppose), but more in giving you a third-person perspective. How often do they meet? How involved is the supervisor? Do they create topics, methodologies and narratives together, or does the supervisor only look at already finished concepts and critique them? Do they meet you once a month, once a week or only when you have something to show them? Are they laid-back and happy for you to do your thing, or are they very set in their ways, with pre-planned check-ins and little room for negotiation on the supervision style? These are all things which determine how well you and your potential supervisor match.

Let me exemplify this. If you are the type of person who needs a lot of direction at the start, e.g. you'd like to have a clear set of expectations and goals that need to be reached, yet your supervisor wants you to be independent and figure it out yourself as part of the "learning process", well, chances are that that isn't going to work out so well, especially not at the start. If you then communicate to your supervisor that you'd like a bit more support at the start, so you can manage it yourself at the end, yet they're utterly non-receptive to this, you've just got yourself one hell of a mismatch. I'm not saying that this is the end of the world, there are ways around this, such as additional collaborations with other academics or figuring this out together with colleagues and fellow supervisees. It's just that if you could avoid this type of interaction, or even this type of mismatch, it would be beneficial to do so, right?

What I've described above is quite a realistic scenario: there'll be rejection, but there'll also be acceptance. However, for some people, there may just be rejection. You can still do two things in this scenario: cold call or find more people you could apply with. If you decide to make another list of potential supervisors, make sure you revisit your email and your proposal. Are they really tailored enough to the person you're reaching out to? Does it mention their work and impact sufficiently? If not, do it again.

I know that as far as time and energy go, the application process is a BEAST. In addition, and this is very representative of academia as a whole: there's a lot of rejection and more negative than positive feedback.

I hope this chapter helped you out with regard to finding a supervisor, and a supervisor who would be a good fit for you. The main message here: do lots of research and collate information from lots of different sources. Once you've solved finding a supervisor let's move onto the next beast: finding funding.

Finding Funding

On top of all the hard work you've already done finding yourself a topic, a place or even several places, to study that topic and several people to study that topic with, you will now have to make sure you also get paid for your time and effort. Yes, it's time to look into securing funding.

To get back to our hot call/cold call distinction, there are some small differences here again: with hot calling, your potential supervisor can help you write, or can at least edit, your funding applications. Additionally, they can point you in the direction of funding you may never have heard of, or even better; they have funding themselves that can fully or partially support you. When cold calling, you lose out on these advantages.

Although I always think the hot/cold distinction is important, more important for this chapter is that, whichever method you apply, there are several different places to look for funding!

The first place to look for funding is at the institutional level. Do the universities hosting the PhD programs offer any form of compensation? At my own university, you could opt into their funding scheme by ticking a single box during the PhD application itself. It genuinely couldn't have been easier.

Not all funding applications at the institutional level will be this easy. The one at my university doesn't require any additional documentation; it's just tagged onto the application process. Some universities will have additional funding competitions for which you'll have to write slightly different documentation. Don't panic. The documentation needed is incredibly similar to all the prep you've already done for the PhD application itself.

The second place to look is your subject level. Are there any organizations specifically in your field that fund research being done in your topic or even in the field in general? For behavioral science, there is NIBS, the organization which I've already mentioned. NIBS is formed by several universities and as a result quite niche. This is why I support hot calling. You're not likely to find something like NIBS if your supervisor doesn't know them. Also, for some of these organizations, your supervisor will have to be part of the organization for you to even qualify. But don't fret, with some thoughtful keywords jammed into Google, maybe even with some university names behind them, you'll be able to track these funding schemes down just fine. But, as I keep hammering home, it does help if you have a potential supervisor who can help you with this!

The third place to look is at the national level. In the country that you're going to do the PhD, does the government, a government body or a very large network or private funder hand out money specifically for research application? If so, time to apply! This, however, is a slightly different ballgame: a lot of these types of funding are referred to as excellence scholarships. You're going to have to compete for them at a much higher level than all the previously mentioned funding schemes. The reason for this is quite simple: the entire country is competing, and they're often not topic or field-specific.

In the UK, where I've been based, they have the ESRC scholarship program, although I'm pretty sure it's been renamed to the UKRI. These abbreviations don't really matter. What matters is that they fund PhD research at the national level for every university in that partnership. And I'm not exaggerating when I say that I'm pretty sure at least 80% of UK universities, if not all of them, are affiliated with this partnership. For these types of funding, as I've mentioned before, competition is steep. Everyone and their mom is applying to them, so you'll need to "level up" your research proposal in terms of its academic rigor, uniqueness and especially its impact. How is your research going to contribute to the world? How is it in line with the goals of the funding scheme you're applying to? A lot of these funding schemes do have an agenda and a couple of key goals they want to achieve for that year or even decade. Make sure you find out what those are and tailor your documents accordingly!

Remaining on the national level, there is also a third-and-a-half place to look: your home country. If you're going abroad to do your PhD, would your own country support you? I had several colleagues of mine, notably from some South American countries, who had their PhD paid for by their respective governments. It seems like the idea of sending citizens abroad, most notably to the UK and the US, for doing their PhD is something those governments are quite happy to pay for, under several conditions, such as an ensured return to your home country to benefit the economy. Which seems fair.

As we've been discussing funding schemes, we've been going up the ladder in terms of scale. However, for the fourth level, we jump down to the smallest level imaginable in this scenario: a single person. If you're hot calling, ask your potential supervisor(s) if they have a pot of money lying around. This is often the case if the PhD position you signed up for is part of a larger grant already. If they didn't have the money to hire a PhD student, the position wouldn't be available. Additionally, the potential supervisor(s) might just have received a large grant without direct purpose (yes they exist); in that case, they might be able to still fund you, with less restrictions as to what your research topic ought to be. The latter is not often an option, but it does happen, so make sure to always check!

Lastly, there is another way of getting funding for the PhD, but it's very specific and won't be as general as the advice I've mentioned so far. The fifth level would be what's referred to as an industry PhD. This is a type of PhD where you've worked for a company for a prolonged period of time, and they're funding the PhD for you, granted that you're doing the PhD in a topic which is relevant to the company. They're paying for research, while keeping a large chunk of it in-house. Additionally, the PhD student in this position continues to work part-time for the company or will have to fulfill some additional requirements to make it worthwhile to the company. Like I said, this is not incredibly common, because you need to have built up a lot of reports with a company already for them to even consider this. So, if you do have an industry background or have been considering a more practical PhD, this is definitely a way of going about it. The funding is definitely a nice touch: it's often higher than PhD student funding because when working for a company, they need to pay a competitive wage for a job rather than a PhD.

These funding schemes as described above are the main ones I can think of with regard to where money normally comes from when doing a PhD. But there are a couple of key facts that I think still need mentioning before finishing this chapter.

Not all funding schemes will cover the whole of your PhD. The cost of a PhD is not a single pot of money; often it's split into several: tuition, stipend and research costs.

You still need to pay tuition, despite being a researcher rather than a taught student (I know…). A lot of funding schemes will cover the tuition fees by default, but that might be it. Tuition fees depend on the university you're working at and whether you're a home or a foreign student. The latter is another thing to check for: some funding schemes only fund home tuition fees. They don't care if you're a foreign student; they're not making up the difference.

With regard to stipend, most funding schemes fund this too, but make sure this is explicitly stated as well. Not all stipend is good stipend. There is the cost of living to consider. Most university schemes have adjusted for this, because they know how much living in that university's area costs. However, field-specific and national schemes might not take this into account. This is again something to consider.

Last, research costs, or a more general research budget. This pot of money consists of a lot more than you'd initially expect. There is of course the cost of doing the research, meaning participant fees, equipment cost, computational power hire (like Amazon web services), research assistants, etc. That's pot one. Pot two is training costs. Will you go on summer schools, take additional courses and other training? If so, who will pay for that? Because that often isn't free either. Pot three is conference costs. During a PhD, attending conferences is a must. Regardless of whether they're online or in real life, they cost money. Conference fees are the main cost, but if you have to attend the conference, there'll be travel and staying costs as well.

Often, the university has these pots of money set up for their PhD students, and this can be complemented by other funding as well, from either the supervisor or a network scheme (NIBS has funded quite a few conferences for me, whereas I could have received money from either Warwick or the ESRC as well).

Having mentioned that sidenote. You can "mix and match". I had two funding schemes: ESRC for my tuition and Warwick for my stipend. The ESRC paid for conferences and additional training, and Warwick paid for some of the research costs out of the standard PhD research allowance. I do have to mention that NIBS paid for most of my research costs, simply because they give research grants. I've received two grants from them. So, all in all, a bit messy, but no lack of money. I'm giving you this example so you don't stare yourself blind on the "all-inclusive" funding schemes. Because guess what? Everyone wants to have those…

Now that I've given you a quick overview of some of the costs to consider when doing a PhD, I hope that you'll have cast the idea of doing a PhD unfunded or only partially funded aside. You're better than that; your work is worth more than that. A PhD is stressful enough without having to worry about making additional money through teaching (TA'ing) or additional research (RA'ing). Don't count on these types of additional sources of income to make ends meet. Please.

Getting Your Documents in Order

Maybe this chapter should've showed up earlier in the book, but I thought it'd be a good idea to actually give you some clear pointers on how to get a lot of the documentation that I keep referring to in order. I've already discussed which documents you're likely to need and their value, so let's dive into some practicalities!

Which documents are you going to need? Well, at the most basic level, you're going to need several of your transcripts (bachelor's and master's), a motivation letter, the reference letters and the much-dreaded research proposal. Let's discuss those in turn.

Your transcripts might not be remotely complete. The UK term starts in October and ends in September. Yet, most of the application deadlines for PhDs fall in December and January. Most institutions are aware of the "lag" between what they're asking for and what you're able to provide. Most of the time, if all the other documents are in order and you have been accepted, you will have been accepted "conditionally". This means that as long as you get grades above a certain level (in the UK this is often above 65% or 70%, referred to as the 2:1), you'll be automatically enrolled into the PhD program. If you fail to get these grades, you won't be. The only real tip I can give here is to keep your transcripts where you can retrieve them and get good grades. That's all really.

Next, the motivation letter. Motivation letters come 13 to a dozen. They've got quite a standard format, which you can google: it has to outline who you are, why you want the PhD (future plans) and why you would be a good fit (topic, skillset, practice, experience, etc.). It's worth it to have this letter checked by multiple of your peers/colleagues. And when I say checked, I mean combed through with a toothpick. It can't be too long or too short or too standard. Like I said, these letters come 13 to a dozen, so you're going to need to stand out somehow, and unless you've earned a Nobel Peace Prize before even starting the PhD, your skillset or achievements won't cut the cake, because everyone has those, as they're the minimum requirement. This document is the most indicative of you as a person, so don't judge it too lightly. Luckily, your potential supervisor, given that you're hot calling, will have a lot of experience with these as well.

Continuing on the thread of reflecting you as a person: you'll also need reference letters. Often you'll need about two or three. It's important to get goods ones, but it seems to be much more important in the US than it is anywhere else. These reference letters need to come from either people in, or related to, the topic of the PhD and/or people who you've worked with and know of your research experience. Within some MSc programs, there will be Personal Tutors available to all students, and they might be good reference writers as well. The key here is to not be hesitant to ask for a reference letter. Most academics expect their students to ask for them and are properly trained in writing good ones, so don't worry too much about asking for "too much", it's almost expected.

Also, two things that need to be mentioned about these reference letters. One, don't be surprised if you never get to see your reference letters. Often the submission systems go directly through the referee and not through the applicant, which is you. This is very common and is done to ensure fairness. Second, don't be surprised if your referee wants, and needs, several documents to be able to even write a good reference letter. The bare minimum you'll need to provide them with is your CV, your motivation letter, the proposal and the PhD position description (if there's one). They'll be able to tailor their letters, increasing the chances of you being accepted into the program. Good referees tailor their letters!

Last, but probably most importantly, you'll have to write a research proposal. The research proposal is a much more rigid format, in which you'll have to outline your research plans for the duration of the PhD. You will have to show a deep understanding of the topic, the method(s) being used and to some extent the analysis.

As has become clear from the quick description above, you're going to have to do a literature review, identify the gaps in the literature and indicate how you're going to address these gaps. You addressing these gaps will have to outline the definition of the gap (what is your research question?) and the methodology for closing the gap. One aspect of the methodology is also the analysis, meaning: is this a quantitative or qualitative approach? What will you measure and how will those variables be analyzed statistically (assuming there's statistics involved). Next, and quite importantly, you'll need to show your planning. When are you doing which part of the project? There seems to be a lot of hype surrounding Gantt charts, so I'm just advising you to make one of those. No joke. This part of the research proposal is used to see whether you're under- or overplanning and whether your research is feasible within the time span indicated.

I've outlined the standard research proposal setup, but make sure to google the format for your specific field or university. They might give tips or entire formats, and if they do, these obviously take precedence over what you've just read.

I've mentioned this before but I'll mention it again: if you're applying without a supervisor, you tend to get matched to one on the basis of your research proposal. If you're applying with a supervisor, they'll often help you write out this proposal, or at least give good advice, improving much of its quality. This is yet another argument to have reached out to potential supervisors way before even starting this application process.

In addition to the "basic" documents I've just described, there may be additional documentation required. Things that I've seen being asked for, but not on a consistent basis, are CVs and several statements, such as teaching and diversity statements.

Your CV should be pretty straightforward. It needs to list all your experience and achievements. It needs to sell you like you've never been sold before. Luckily, there are loads of online tutorials for CV writing and lots of online templates that can help you craft the best CV humanly possible. Do make use of these; they're out there for a reason.

Teaching and diversity statements are a slightly different batch. The former wants to know about your previous experience, if you have any, or how excited you are about teaching and what type of teacher you're likely to be. The latter wants to know whether you are remotely diverse (non-male, non-binary, non-hetero, non-white, non-country-you're-going-to-do-the-PhD-in (so foreign), non-neurotypical, non-student-age or have any type of recognized disability). Work with that list to the best of your ability, because the admissions team really does care about this. If you literally do not qualify for any of the aforementioned, indicate how you've contributed to helping those who do qualify for anything on that list. Charity work always does well, especially in the US.

I'm sure there is other documentation that you may need for your PhD application, but these would be the most frequently asked for. When in doubt, or faced with something you're really not too sure of, google it. It sounds stupid but it works like a charm. There's no way on earth that you're going to be the very first and the only person dealing with something confusing during the PhD application process. There've been others before you, and they've taken to the Internet to help out others. So, profit of that knowledge and prepare your documentation accordingly!

How to Survive an Interview

Assuming that your documentation was well in order and you've progressed to the next stage, you may or may not be asked to interview. And you need to prep for that too.

Now, I say that you may or may not be asked to interview because not all universities have this system in place. And even universities that do have these systems in place don't interview everyone (they might interview external applicants but not internal ones). So, this chapter may not be equally relevant to all of you, but I thought I'd include it, just to be sure.

When going for the interview, you've already got one arm and a leg in the door. Clearly, you're qualified because otherwise you wouldn't have made it this far. Universities that run interview rounds want to see if you're a fit beyond your skills and qualifications. The latter now having simply become a "ticked box".

To see if you're a good fit is mainly an elaboration on your motivational statement and to some extent the research proposal. They want to see if you're actually serious about your research, whether you're excited about your research and whether you have the "right" motivation for doing the PhD. In this interview, you need to sell yourself verbally rather than textually.

For some people, this is a breeze. For others, this is a nightmare. If you're any good at public speaking, this will be easier than if you're not. But fret not, there are tips and tricks for this as well.

As I've mentioned before, this interview is to elaborate. So dive into what they already know from your documentation and sell it even more. Go into depth more, paint the picture and tell the story. Don't make these things up on the spot either. You know what's in your statements (and on your CV, if submitted), so do they. Don't suddenly come up with entirely new experiences that your interviewers cannot verify!

Another aspect of the interview is that they may give you sets of questions which can be best described as circumstantial, and I don't mean the type of evidence. They might ask you what you'd do in certain circumstances regarding your research or your teaching. This type of stuff is highly infrequent.

If you're worried about the interview process, reach out to current PhD students at the universities you're interested in pursuing a PhD at. I keep giving this advice but it's worth repeating: they've already been through what you're currently going through, and they've been through it recently. They have the most up-to-date information there is. So make use of that!

Offers and Rejections

Interview or no interview, CV or no CV submission, cold or hot calling. More likely than not, you'll receive both rejections and hopefully some, if only just one, offer. After all, it's only one you need.

Unless you're the best PhD candidate ever, you're going to get some rejections. This is not a reflection on you, this just is. I don't think I've ever heard of anyone with a 100% application success rate, unless they simply applied to one university and hoped for the best, probably through already knowing their potential supervisors.

As I've said before, some strategies do have higher success rates than others. I don't like cold applications, and applications at the same university where you did one of your previous degrees have a higher success rate as well. Knowing this, you can adjust accordingly.

If you've been very successful and you've received multiple offers, you have a choice. You now need to make a cost–benefit analysis for all the programs you've gotten into and choose what's best for you. How you prioritize different aspects of the PhD (supervisor, topic, methodology, funding, prestige, location, cost of living, etc.) is entirely up to you and does depend on your individual circumstance. The only thing I can really give advice on, from personal experience, is to make sure you pick a supervisor that works well for you, a topic you can at least maintain vague interest in for a prolonged period of time and a program/funding scheme that fully covers your expenses. Those were the most important aspects for me. You might not care about these at all. Whichever way you end up choosing your program, I congratulate you on your offers and wish you the best in your PhD.

When you've only received one offer, there's no cost–benefit analysis to be had, really. You have an offer, so let's go! Unless, you're not happy with the offer for some reason. Maybe the university that accepted you wasn't even in your top 5 or the funding doesn't fully cover you. The question then becomes: do you still want to do the PhD? I don't think asking yourself this question when you're experiencing a lot of negative emotions, due to the rejections you might have already received, is smart, but it's a question you'll quite likely ask yourself anyway. A clever way around this is to not apply to any PhD programs you wouldn't be happy with from the start. This might sound risky to some, but why would you waste time applying to places and programs you don't want to be in? The application process is very time consuming, so choose wisely.

So, if you have applied to quite a few programs and you've only been accepted to programs, or a single program, that you don't want to do, should you still do it? This becomes a question of opportunity cost. Can you do something else in the several years it'll take completing this PhD you don't seem to want? The answer to that is yes. You can do many things that aren't PhD programs. But the real question is whether these other opportunities are better than the PhD program you've been accepted to. You could also try again next year and need to find something to do in the meantime, like work for a year or gain relevant experience for the PhD through being a research assistant. The choice is yours, just make sure you're really considering all relevant factors here. If you still decide to do the PhD because it's actually a great opportunity and you realize that the only reason you were down about it was because of the monumental amount of rejections you had already received, then I still congratulate you on your offer and your journey into the PhD.

Having already mentioned them, it's time to discuss them in much more depth: rejections. As I said before, it's likely you're going to receive some rejections.

If you've received nothing but rejections, that sucks. After a short period of anger, sadness, grief or all of the above, try to get your head back in the game. See if you can get feedback on your applications. It's important to know why you were rejected. Do you lack the right qualifications? It's possible your degrees aren't a good fit for what you're trying to do. It's also possible you're aiming for top universities whereas your grades might not indicate that you're a top student. The admissions committee do check for that quite ferociously. Are you experienced enough? If not, would you be willing to get more research experience as a research assistant to make up for it? Being a research assistant to a research group you'd want to work in or to a person you'd want to work for is actually a very common way of progressing into a PhD, but it does cost more time. A lot of people do also do this during their bachelor's or master's degree, but this obviously indicates a longer-term plan.

Whatever the reason for your rejections may be, try to figure it out and adjust accordingly. Edit your documents, reach out to more potential supervisors and reach out to different research groups and universities until you have an offer. Or, if you've been completely demoralized, which is very understandable, check if the PhD is really for you. If you receive feedback which means you'd have to go into a drastically different direction to even be considered, with additional training and experience to be acquired, are you sure you want to do it? Maybe look into different fields and topics for doing your PhD. Maybe drop the idea altogether. I'm not saying you should quit just because you've received rejections. Most of the PhD is a long chain of different forms of rejections and negative feedback. But if the answer to the same question is always no, something is clearly not working. And you need to figure out what isn't working before you keep repeating the same trick again and again, with the same result. Just some advice.

A quick note I want to end this chapter on: a lot of offers are *conditional* offers, meaning that you're going to have to satisfy a set of criteria before you're allowed to actually start the PhD. The most common condition is to finish your current degree with a certain accreditation, such as the UK's 2:1 (60–69%) or a first (>70%), or the US's minimum of a B or 3.0 GPA.

Now, these are standard requirements, but we all know that admissions prefer someone who's got firsts all the way through, as compared to someone who's struggling to reach a 2:1, unless you've got quite a lot of additional qualifications and experience standing next to those grades. And this leads to a much larger overarching point: being an ideal candidate. If you know you want to do a PhD really early on, you're at an advantage, because you can tailor your entire existence to the requirements of your PhD program of your choice. But this is by no means the only way to get into a PhD or even the most successful strategy. So don't get too carried away.

Concluding Remarks

In this section, I've done my best to outline how to go about finding a topic, a university, a supervisor and funding. Well, actually, I've told you how to find multiple of those, because I'm afraid most people don't manage the one-shot-goal.

What I've hoped to do here is show you how much work PhD applications are, or should be, without trying to scare you off. If it makes you feel any better, applying to industry-based jobs can be just as tedious: they might have less paperwork (sometimes it's just as bad), but what they lack in written statements they make up for in interviews. Several rounds of tedious interviews (this is currently a sensitive topic for me).

Please don't be alarmed by the amount of work these applications are. If you're serious about doing a PhD, you should've seen this coming already. PhD programs are becoming increasingly more competitive as more and more people want to do PhDs. This is a trend that's been on the rise for a long time now. As a result, you need to prepare accordingly.

If there's anything I'd like you to take away from this chapter, it's to hot call rather than to cold call, to do a lot of preparation before even starting your application and to very carefully craft your application, with a strong focus on the research proposal.

I won't be surprised if you'll end up having to email at least 20 potential supervisors to only be accepted by two of them who'll actively help you. I won't be surprised if you'll end up having to write multiple versions, more than five at least, of your research proposal, as well as your motivational or personal statement, to fit the requirements.

This will be a very time-consuming project that you'll have to integrate into your probably already very busy life. Whether you're already working or still studying, doing PhD applications can feel like a full-time job. Make sure you have the right people around you to support you powering through it. I'm sure you'll be fine.

And once you've made it into the PhD, well, then the next sections of this book will become very relevant to you! Good luck.

Section 3

Starting the PhD!

And here we are. You've done the groundwork, done all the applications, made the connections, faced the rejections and at last, you have arrived at a PhD program!

As you start the first day of your PhD, how do you feel? Excited? Nervous? Ready to go? A bit worried maybe? Not too sure what to expect yet? Whichever way you're feeling, it's completely valid. Do me a favor and savor however you're currently feeling and congratulate yourself on the milestone you've just reached. It's important to savor and celebrate. Trust me.

Now, this section of the book is where things get a bit more wobbly. Wobbly in a sense that my PhD was 4 years, and I was planning to take you through that journey, and the massive themes that arose within those 4 years. However, that greatly reduces the usefulness of this book, as my PhD is clearly not your PhD. I was in what's known as a 1+3 program, where the first year is still largely taught, and there is no real expectation of you doing research. Some people will have a similar first year, or even first years, as some programs are more like a 2+4, where the initial 2 years are taught and need to be fully passed before moving onto the research part of the PhD. This is quite common for the American system and those who study economics.

So, knowing how different the systems are, the titles of this section are getting a bit more vague. I will talk more about general trends that I expect you to face at the start of the PhD and will make sure to indicate why I think you'll be facing this and why I'm talking about it in this section.

You won't be surprised to find that Chapter 15 on coursework still refers to the taught part of the PhD and that as we progress in this section, the chapters will focus much more on the research part of the PhD, which you'll increasingly become involved in as the PhD progresses, even at the very start.

Although my PhD is not your PhD, I did include my own experiences at the very end of this section. For the blog, I've always written an annual review for each year of the PhD and thought including the one I wrote regarding my first year might be helpful or at least somewhat relatable for you.

Without much further ado, let's jump into all the things to look out for during the start of your PhD!

Settling in

There will be a period of readjustment. You've probably just moved to a different place to be able to do your PhD. Whether that's as simple as moving from one end of the city to the other or from one end of the world to the opposite side of it, there will have been a transition. There will have been changes.

Change is not a bad thing if you know how to handle it. With regard to this, I actually recommend, although possibly a bit late now, that you give yourself time to settle in. Don't move house on a Sunday and then have to start the PhD program on the Monday after. That's a bit much. Unless you live that work-hard-play-harder lifestyle. You do you.

Anyway, back to the changes. You've probably moved locations, and you'll have to move mental states as well. If you've always been in education, the initial transition to the PhD should not be too hardcore. The first year(s) is often still taught, which helps with smoothening over the transition, as you're used to being taught, meeting short-term deadlines and having the resources to do so provided to you. If you've come back from industry and haven't been taught in a while, this transition is a bit rougher. Back in lecture seats, probably surrounded by quite a few people who are a bit, if not a lot, younger than you are. Constant studying, I've been told, is very different from working a job, so do prepare for a slightly rockier road. And keep in mind that your memories of education will probably be completely rose-colored and also no longer up to date!

Another transition to focus on might be a financial transition. If you've been exclusively in education beforehand without ever working full-time jobs, this might mean that suddenly you have a much larger income. When I say much larger, I just mean that any increase from zero is large. The wage, or rather stipend, from a PhD is really underwhelming, and depending on the country and system you're in, it might not actually be minimum wage when offset against the hours worked.

This transition is again going to be rough for those coming back to academia from industry, especially if you've held a high-paying job. However, if you did have a high-paying job, you had the time to build a buffer for the years of economic scarcity to come. Which is obviously not something most people coming straight out of education had time to do. Whichever way you're approaching your financial situation, both current and past, I hope you focused on this well enough in Section 1 of this book for it to no longer be a massive issue.

As you can see here from describing the location, mindset and financial transition, there tend to be quite a few differences between those coming straight from education and those who've held down jobs in the meantime. This is a difference that'll mainly persist at the start and might completely fade out as you move further into the PhD. It needn't fade out, as the PhD is a highly individual experience to begin with. So, it can honestly go any possible way.

Another aspect of settling in, which is very important, is how you should go about settling in socially. PhD programs do tend to have a start date which is in line with the rest of the academic year. So, when you arrive, so does everyone else (undergraduates, postgraduates, etc.). This means all the activities are catered towards this well. Think of attending some of these to get a better feel for the university at which you're now residing, as well as figuring out if there are any social or sports associations you'd like to join. University, even at the PhD level, is a massively social experience as well. And don't think you're too old for this. If you have the time to have a social life, I would strongly recommend it!

Again, if you're a more mature PhD student, this might be less appealing, but I wouldn't write it off completely. If you have a family next to doing your PhD or even part-time work still, I can imagine you might not be super interested in attending socials or matches with people who've just left the parental nest. Fair enough. It really depends on what stage of life you're in to warrant this type of settling in.

Of course, most of the above advice is not super useful for those who stayed at their alma mater and did so on purpose. To do your postgraduate degree (master's) at the same university you want to do your PhD is a good strategy, from both a strategic perspective, as well as a settling-in perspective. Be nice about it and help new PhD students settle in, and help each other out that way!

Coursework

Now, let's actually dive into an aspect of the PhD some people would rather not talk about: the coursework. Yes, it's very unlikely you can get away with doing no coursework at all during the PhD. Some people will have years of taught modules and some people will have to sporadically fulfill a course credit requirement to have enough credits to pass the PhD as a whole. Whichever way it is, there the PhD program is likely to have a taught element.

Wobble alert: if you don't have a taught aspect to your PhD at all, which is entirely possible although not likely, you can skip this chapter! However, do check that you have no course credit requirements AT ALL. I'll explain more about this in this chapter (yes, this was one of the mistakes I made…).

Let's assume, which is statistically very likely, that the initial part of your PhD is taught and that you've got at least a year of this. This means several things: the focus is on the modules rather than your own research; there are short-term deadlines to meet; this part is highly structured and you need to fit your work into that structure. This might not feel like you are actually doing a PhD.

Now, I won't spend too much time on talking you through the actual courses or the work associated with them. Anyone who's in a PhD program has at least done an undergraduate degree, and knows how to sit in lectures and take notes. Some of these courses will be useful to you, some of these won't. Some of them will be super-repetitive, others won't make any sense to you and you'll never revisit its contents again. You might be able to select some of these courses yourself, or the journey has been entirely planned out for you. Whichever way this goes, you're just going to have to get through them.

Unsurprisingly, this is where a lot of people experience their initial disappointment. Why is this not surprising? Well, this is nothing like what doing a PhD is. To some, this entire taught aspect might feel like a massive distraction from the research they came to do.

My advice in this regard is rather simple: if you can pick courses, pick the ones that are most useful to you. If possible, even do courses at other departments if that helps you in the slightest. Courses to really look out for are those that help you master your methodology of choice. If you're grounded in statistics, take some econometrics and computer science courses. This just casts your net wider, might give you some additional insights and will help you in the long run. I think taking methods courses is preferred to taking topical courses, granted that you're not massively interested in these topical courses or actually lack topical knowledge which these courses could supplement you with.

If you cannot pick your courses, you just need to put up with that. I don't often tell people to just put up with something. I'm exactly the type of person to try to figure out how many ways there are to get around something rather than doing it, but with this one, it's more efficient to just plow through.

Also, there's the advice we generally got given by our supervisors: get the grades required to pass the courses, and move on. They quite explicitly state to do the bare minimum. If you can live with that, do it. Issue is, most PhD students are massive overachievers, so I get it if you'd rather pass with 70% (a first, an A, an 8/10 or cum laude). In some institutions, these taught years do actually end up being a formal degree rather than just a prerequisite, and some people don't want any "blemishes" on their educational records, and that's a completely valid line of reasoning. So you decide how much time you want to spend on these courses, and study accordingly. And don't let anyone else tell you differently!

To close this chapter, let's move onto the mistakes I made during the PhD. There were two with regard to coursework that I think that deserve to be highlighted, so you won't make them.

First mistake: I had no idea my taught year was going to be a formal degree (MA Social Science Research), which required another dissertation. I came into the PhD having done an MSc in Behavioural and Economic Science. Obviously, an MSc requires a dissertation at the end of it (in the UK system). I quite enjoyed doing that dissertation; it actually functioned as a pilot for the very first study I did in my PhD, so that worked out well.

However, as I was taking courses in the first (taught) year of my PhD both together with my ESRC cohort (tuition funding) and my WBS cohort (stipend funding), things started to move out of sync. Whereas the WBS cohort was talking about the Upgrade (pass–fail review board for looking at your progress in year 1), the ESRC cohort was talking about their dissertation. Dissertation?! It turned out these two systems weren't remotely compatible (it makes you wonder how they did this in previous years because neither of the systems is new…). For the WBS Upgrade, you were required to have your full literature review and research planning in order. For the ESRC dissertation, you had to pick a whole new topic because you couldn't plagiarize that dissertation for your PhD. Great…

In the end, I was able to repurpose some of the data from my very first study. The study itself was about the effect of different payment methods on immediate expenditure recall. I repurposed those data to write a dissertation on price prominence, a completely different topic which required quite a lot of additional reading and writing. In the end, I passed this dissertation with a first and as a result, the formal degree with a first as well, so all is well that ends well. But without having had those data ready, I'm not too sure what I would've done… What should you take away from my mistake? Read your contract carefully. Or more likely in your PhD: be fully aware of the requirements of the coursework. Check with the administrative staff that your information is up to date and you know fully what is expected of you. And act accordingly!

Second mistake: I had no idea that I had to get more course credit throughout the PhD itself. I realized way too late into my PhD contract that on top of the additional MA degree, I'd also have to collect 20 course credits throughout the PhD. I realized this in February of my final year due to an off-chance conversation with one of my collaborators. My thesis was due in September, and time was running out! Luckily, the requirement was set by the ESRC, which spans universities all over the UK, which means

I could take the courses at any university, at any given time. By this stage, all courses were also still online and had been adapted to the online format. This meant I could quickly do two courses, both at 10 credits, to satisfy this requirement. I did a course on Policy Evaluation and one on Time Series Regression. I can't claim they were super interesting to me, but they were available to me at the University of Birmingham, at a time which was convenient to me (end of May, early June), and could easily be fit into my work schedule. As far as this mistake goes, it could've ended a lot worse!

So, what should you take away from these mistakes? Again, read your contract and all its requirements carefully and plan accordingly! And if it turns out you did miss something, get creative to make it work. It would have been much more beneficial to me had I been able to choose courses on statistical analysis, experimental design, programming, etc. given that I had to do coursework anyway. But that didn't happen, because I didn't know I had to do more additional coursework. So be sure to check ALL requirements.

Planning the Research

Despite being in the taught part of your PhD, this doesn't mean that the research should be ignored. There'll be the general expectation that as soon as the taught aspect ends, you'll be ready to go and hit the ground running in terms of starting your research. This means you've already refined your methods, based on the prior literature, which you have read and written up entirely.

Within the UK system specifically, you're expected to at least have your literature review finished when coming out of the taught aspect of your PhD. This is also why you need to have this ready for the aforementioned Upgrade. So, there are expectations with regard to research, even in the taught aspect of your PhD.

Now, how much research planning is required during the taught aspect of your PhD, assuming you have a taught aspect? Well, this obviously does depend on the length of the taught aspect, but there are some general pointers, which seem to not vary much per institution. As mentioned before, you need a literature review. You might be thinking: "have I not done this already for my research proposal?" You have. About 10% of it.

When you start your PhD, you will have proper access to your supervisor(s). They should be able to now seriously look at what you're planning to do and invest their time accordingly. It's entirely possible that through multiple discussions or simply a change in context (time does elapse between your proposal and you actually starting the PhD program), there will be a change in PhD topic or method. Several of my colleagues have had this happen to them, and so have I. You start off with one idea and end up with something different entirely. This is completely fine but will require some rewriting and replanning.

So, after multiple talks with your supervisor(s), what direction is your PhD taking? What resources are available to you? What are the interests of your supervisor(s)? Where can you find common ground? Again, you're probably thinking that you've already been through all of this when creating the research proposal. But there's a difference between writing this proposal and actually doing the research. Your supervisor(s) is now much more invested. This will likely lead to changes. Changes that will need to be evaluated against some restrictions with regards to feasibility, finance, time and other resources available.

It needs to be mentioned though that this amount of wiggle room is normal for an unstructured PhD, whereas it's a lot less likely in PhD programs for which the methods were already established. For more on the distinctions between those types of PhDs, go back to Section 1.

When you're planning the research, topics, methods and timeframes will start to take form. By the way, this is not a quick process, this will take months, not weeks. Just letting you know so you can adjust your expectations accordingly. Final goals and steps towards those goals will start to form. For the topic, you'll start to refine the gaps in the literature, the methodologies that have been used before and are judged as appropriate for the exact research questions you're aiming to answer, if those methodologies even already exist. Through this, you'll start building your first study or first chapter if you'd rather call it that. Although it's more like your third chapter, as the introduction and literature review are Chapters 1 and 2, most likely. Anyway…

You'll be refining the days away, your supervisor(s) will give you helpful pointers with regards to reading more literature, figuring out how to approach certain topics and research questions, which methods to use and refining those methods as well. It's entirely possible that you'll have to train further methodological knowledge and skills to be able to do your PhD; this is why I suggest looking into courses like that if you can.

Also, there'll be some administrative rump slump to deal with during this process. Unless the PhD was super structured from the get-go, there'll be ethical and financial considerations, at the very least. When working with animals, people or dangerous substances (chemistry, medicine), you'll need to jump through several ethical hoops to even be allowed to do this. And as those aforementioned become more threatened (animals), vulnerable (people) or more dangerous (substances), there'll be even more hoops. Your department will have processes in place for this, but it'll still take a lot of time. Obviously, there's a good reason for why these processes are in place; just look up the Milgram (1963) electrocution study and you'll get my vibe. Just plan for this part of the research to take up some time.

Looking at this from another perspective: when working with companies and their data, there'll very likely be a variety of Non-Disclosure Agreements (NDAs) to sign. If these companies have these procedures in place already, thanks to their legal team, this shouldn't be too much of an issue. If you and your university/department have to be onboarded, this is a very lengthy process. Bear this in mind!

With regard to getting your finances in order, I'm exclusively referring to the finances required for your research, not for you as a researcher. To put it quite frank: who's paying for this stuff?

If you're working with substances or any materials really, where are they coming from? Do they need to be ordered? How do they need to be ordered and from which budget? Maybe your supervisor(s) has a budget for this, maybe the department does, maybe you do. But it would be good to know!

The same goes for animal research, especially if the animals require training. Who's training them or more economically, who's being paid to train them and what will it cost? If it's you, I doubt there's additional payment for it, but it'll cost you time. Do you have that time or can you afford to employ someone to do this for you? Also, if these animals are being sacrificed in the name of science, what additional costs are related to this? It's incredibly expensive to order, train, keep and correctly dispose of research animals.

With people, this works a bit differently, because you tend to not be allowed to melt them down or cage them. But for participation in studies on behavior or medication, for example, you still need to compensate them accordingly. Same questions with regard to budgeting apply.

It's also entirely possible that your PhD focuses on creation and invention. In that case, although ethics and finances are still considerations to be had, you also need to figure out intellectual property rights and financial rewards of the invention itself, and you need to figure them out before even signing the PhD contract. A lot of universities, or organizations in general, will suddenly become very pesky and petty when you try to claim something as your own, given how much support they've given you in your PhD. There have been lawsuits regarding this, so watch your back.

As I've mentioned before, all of this will somehow be expected to happen next to your coursework. So, it's a bit of a juggling act. It's true that *technically* speaking your focus should be on your coursework, but it's also entirely true that the coursework doesn't benefit your supervisor(s) in any way and that the incentives of where the focus should be are perpendicular to each other. It's important to make enough time for properly planning your research so that when the research aspect of your PhD comes, you're ready to go. However, as I've said before, if you want to finish your courses with proper grades, especially if they constitute another formal degree, that is fair too. You just need to communicate this to your supervisor(s) properly.

On the topic of communication: there is another massive reason for why I'd recommend immediately starting meetings with your supervisor(s) as well as start planning research and working together. It doesn't matter that you're still in the taught part of your PhD. As I said before, you're going to have to hit the ground running, and you need help doing that.

So why do you need to meet your supervisor(s) early on? You'll find out quite quickly if you're actually compatible. Which is exactly what I want to discuss in the next chapter.

My Supervisor and I

A lot of research went into figuring out who the right supervisor for you was. You'd think that by that stage you'd be done, but nothing could be further from the truth. You now have to figure out how to actually work together, as a team.

This will involve figuring out several things: how do they work? How do you like to work? Are there common grounds? Are they letting you talk? Do you have any say or input in discussions or are they simply treating you as a research assistant, telling you what to and when? And if so, is that okay with you, given that you're still at the very start? How do you want this relationship to progress? And what are your expectations from them as a supervisor?

Okay, don't panic. I know I went a bit haywire there, and there is a lot to unpack, but there are nice and easy ways of doing it. The key? Communication!

It's possible, even quite likely, that your supervisor has been supervising PhDs for years, if not decades by now. This means they'll have their own style of supervising and probably have tailored this to be what works best for them. Especially if they are supervising quite a few students at the same time, this is very likely.

Now, this can go one of two ways: either it's working for you or it isn't. It's probably better to figure this out sooner rather than later. As soon as you start meeting regularly, and I would like to emphasize that this should still happen during the taught part of your PhD, ask them what their style is. How often do they normally meet PhD students? What do they expect from their meetings? Some of my colleagues met their supervisors on a monthly basis and had to have presentations ready to update their supervisors of their progress and any issues they may have encountered. I met my supervisors on an almost weekly basis and just talked them through what was going on and asked for advice on any issues. Some of the advice they had to give me was incredibly hands-on, as in, literally helping me code up the analysis because things weren't working. As our relationship progressed, which it will over several years, we got to a stage where I asked for less advice and just updated them on things that had happened and whether I needed them to do something, like read and edit certain chapters, schedule meetings with collaborators, etc.

As I said, your relationship will progress. At least it should. You'll get to know each other better and figure out what works best for the both of you. Granted, if something isn't working, you should indicate this honestly, and respectfully, and hope that you've signed up to a supervisor who cares to hear your thoughts and does actively want the best for you. If this is not the case, you might want to consider your options in dealing with this situation and potentially switching supervisor(s).

What I've described above might come across as a bit passive. You're asking your supervisor about them and their working style rather than actively asserting yours. Well, if you feel comfortable asserting your own working style and you actually know your own working style, great, go for it. I don't see any issue with it and I do think this type of clarity can be very useful. However, I can imagine that not everyone is comfortable with doing this. Also, if it turns out your expectations are very different from your supervisors with regard to meeting frequency, investment in the PhD and week-to-week progress, well, that'll be another discussion point in and of itself. Not necessarily a bad one, I'm just giving you a heads up!

Now, if your supervisor is a whole new person to you and you had no real relationship with them before they onboarded you as their supervisee, I can imagine that sitting down with them and blurting out your preferred working style is just a bit more than you settled for, which is why give the general advice to figure it out together and see where you end up.

I've already mentioned before that this discussion will lead to an agreement that either works for you or it doesn't. If it doesn't, just tell your supervisor. Figure out together what aspect of your agreement isn't working. Maybe you don't see the value in presenting them with an entire PowerPoint presentation every month. Maybe you want to meet more frequently. Maybe there are aspects of the PhD that you need more hands-on help with. Or maybe you don't see the point in meeting regularly and would rather just reach out whenever you need help. All of these things are fair and should be up for discussion. If your supervisor is not up for discussing any of these or remotely changing their ways to help you out, we have a problem. Again, consider your options. Would taking on an additional supervisor help? Or do you need to find a different supervisor altogether?

Another important aspect of communication is how you communicate. And with how I mainly mean via what platform. Initially, I emailed my supervisors. That is essentially the default. However, one of my supervisors got so many emails in a day that my email simply got lost in the endless stream of things he had to do. He decided that it would be easier to talk in a more direct way, which in our case was via WhatsApp. Interestingly enough, my other supervisor wasn't too keen on the idea, and I fully understand why but had to give in to accommodate the supervisory unit.

The solution for this is also rather easy. We're in a group chat in which we only discuss work. If I only need something from the "first" supervisor, I send him a message via WhatsApp. If I only need something from the "second" supervisor, I'll just email him. He's actually very good over email.

On top of workstyle differences, there might also be differences in personality or attitude. It's very likely that your supervisor(s) and you won't have the same personality. It'd be much more shocking if you did, actually.

So, let's imagine that your attitudes just don't match. They are very relaxed about it all (having done it before), and you are ripping your hair out to relieve your own anxiety as you're new to it all. That's obviously not ideal, but given that this is a very personal trait, ingrained in the person that they are, there might not be too much you can change there. If you're naturally anxious, it is probably a good idea to learn how to relax more and see things in a different perspective. But, you can hardly ask your supervisor to be more stressed for you. If their "relaxedness" really does bother you, you can indicate this to them. You might perceive it as a disregard for your own worries or a lack of care for your research or you as a person. Again, be honest. But don't expect them to change an attitude which is very much part of their personality. They're only human after all.

Another mismatch which I've seen is the sense of humor. Some people find a lot of things funny. They like to start the meetings off with a joke or a funny story of something that has recently happened to them. If you're in those meetings and you just want to get on with work, this may not seem particularly useful to you. If you're actually very stressed about your PhD and the minutes are ticking away while they're building up to their punchline, you might just explode. If this is a very frequent occurrence, you might want to indicate to your supervisor(s) that you'd prefer to make most of the time they give you in these meetings. But you might not want to do this. Why? Well, it might be a cultural thing.

On top of workstyle and personality, there are also cultural differences to consider. And I recommend you consider them well.

The most notable cultural differences in PhD supervision are those relating to hierarchy (if you ask me). Some cultures enforce a very steep hierarchy, others do not. I myself am Dutch (very flat hierarchy) and my supervisors are Italian (flat to medium) and British (flat to semi-flat). This in itself does not pose any issues, and I've always been very thankful for that. Despite a very clear skill level difference, they've always approached me as part of the team rather than the runt. And my Italian supervisor even mentioned towards the end of my final year that I'd be "a colleague of theirs soon" rather than just a PhD student. Well, as you can imagine, that made my day.

But I do know PhD students who come from very hierarchical cultures, who take their supervisors' word as gospel, do everything they say and beat themselves up if this doesn't work or doesn't lead to good results. This is not what a PhD is supposed to be. The PhD research is yours and your supervisor(s) are supposed to support you through it. They should not take over nor sideline you, and you should neither expect this from them nor want this from them. Again, if the PhD is a structured PhD, you knew what you signed up for and doing "your own thing" is just not what that PhD program is about, so keep that in mind. This has nothing to do with your supervisor's culture, that's just the design of the PhD.

The other way round can be true as well: your supervisor shouldn't expect you to blindly follow all of their suggestions and do the research as they say it should be done. Hierarchical or not, this is your project!

Now, it might be difficult to figure out whether they're giving you advice or are trying to take over. But these are not remotely the same thing! Especially at the very start, if you're a bit clueless about what you ought to be doing, asking for advice or being given advice and actually following it is not a bad strategy. It really isn't. But if this advice is taking the shape of always rejecting your ideas and the sentence "I really think you should be doing this instead…" and they've mentioned this repeatedly, it might be a good idea to discuss why they think that. Another thing to discuss is why you seem to be so reluctant to do it, given that you haven't worked on their suggestion yet. Again, even when keeping the potential hierarchical differences in mind, you're entitled to your own opinion and talking openly about your ideas for your research project(s).

It's of course also possible that there are other cultural differences going on. Another notable cultural difference is how the genders interact with and view each other. If you ever feel like your supervisor is disadvantaging you because of your gender (whichever gender that may be), you do need to talk about that. They might be doing it unconsciously. If you've raised this problem and nothing seems to change or things seem to have worsened, you might want to consider switching supervisors and talking to HR as well.

Of course, cultural differences need not be this extreme at all. Most cultural differences are ones you can easily get used to, like the desire to start with a joke or funny store each meeting, and can do some research on to better understand them. Again, if it's causing a rift between you and your supervisor, the best thing to do is to talk about it and go from there. But do so respectfully. Culture is a very sensitive topic.

Now, I do think that if there's clear and honest communication between both parties, most issues can be resolved. However, there are always exceptions to this rule, and they center entirely around any type of very inappropriate behavior. Things that should immediately spring to mind are racism, sexism and abuse of power (in any form). The best thing to do if these scenarios are occurring or have occurred is to immediately talk to someone, preferably someone in charge.

If you're not too sure about what's going on and whether it qualifies as any of the above, talk to your friends and fellow PhD students. If they also don't think what's going is appropriate, talk to someone in charge. If you don't want to directly accuse someone, you can always speak in hypotheticals, change names, etc.

Even if you're not too sure, but feel incredibly uncomfortable, I'd still recommend you step to HR, the head of your research group or the head of your department, whoever you feel most comfortable with. They will be able to advise you on which course of action will be best to take. That decision is ultimately up to you. Again, if you prefer to use hypotheticals, do so.

There's no excuse for this type of behavior. It is not condoned and shouldn't be. There's also no coming back from this. After this has occurred and you still want to continue your research project, under no circumstances should you go back or be made to go back to your original supervisor. Immediate transfer advised. In cases like this, HR is likely to get involved and the switching process will look a bit different from the one I described before, so be wary of this.

I've mentioned switching supervisors a couple of times now and will address it in later chapters as well. But I suppose it would be rather helpful if I outlined for you how this would work, exactly.

Switching supervisors can be, but often isn't, an easy process. If it becomes apparent that your supervisor had very different expectations of you and your PhD in terms of topic or methodology, your interests may not be as compatible as they were originally believed to be and you might both agree on a switch. It's also possible you've decided to slightly change topics or methodology and have made yourself and your work incompatible with your supervisor. It does happen. In this scenario, because the switch isn't for personal reasons and no one is being harmed, this is a rather problem-free type of switch. In this case, because you're likely still on neutral to good terms, your supervisor may help you find a new, more compatible supervisor in the same research group, department or at least university. To stay at the same university in this case is preferred as it's simply easier, especially if the funding comes (mainly) from the university.

Switching supervisors is not always the answer, however. In the previous example, it may be easier to take on an additional supervisor who has more topical or methodological expertise. This causes even less friction and is considered quite normal. Additionally, you can also start different collaborations with people who have whatever your initial supervisor is lacking. Again, really quite common and doesn't ruffle too many feathers. So, if it's mainly a work issue, switching is not always the answer. If you feel like switching would be much more beneficial rather than adding on supervisors or collaborators, it's still a good idea to talk this through with your initial supervisor.

Talking about work issues, it's also possible that your working styles aren't compatible. I've mentioned before that some supervisors don't feel the need to see their supervisees every week or even every month. But if you really need that, well you've got a problem. If you've communicated this clearly to your initial supervisor but they won't budge, you can again take on additional supervisors and collaborators who have much more compatible working styles. This need not be problematic, depending on how things turn out. If you're now meeting your second supervisor weekly and updating your initial supervisor of your progress on a monthly basis, and everyone is okay with this arrangement, that's great. They put in the level of effort they're comfortable with and you get all the support you need. However, this can also completely backfire where the initial supervisor is offended by the idea of you "needing more help" in the form of an additional supervisor and then refuses to continue supervising you. This means that you might be supervisor-less for some time while finding a new supervisor. This is essentially forced switching. Without the help of your initial supervisor, finding a new supervisor takes you all the way back to Chapter 8, where I explained how to look for a good supervisor, for you.

The difference in starting from scratch (Chapter 8) and the current situation would be that you are likely restricted to a single research group, department or university, so your choices have starkly diminished. Still, you're going to have to make the most of your situation. You'll have to reach out again to potential supervisors and get them to onboard you. Not onto the university system this time round but onto their research agenda. If your initial supervisor is the only expert in your topic at a university, this really isn't ideal, and that's putting it lightly. This is why I urge you to put a lot of effort into finding the right supervisor for you.

The two scenarios I described above are essentially problem-free scenarios. They are problem-free as things aren't really personal. Your initial supervisor may even help find you a new supervisor, who is more compatible topic or workstyle wise.

These specific issues in terms of compatibility often arise during the start of the PhD or at least relatively early on. It becomes clear quite quickly whether expectations in terms of topic, output and collaboration (work division) overlap. Or whether they do not overlap at all. Switching supervisors early on in the PhD because of this mismatch is not uncommon and as such not too difficult.

However, don't make the mistake of thinking that switching supervisors is a super easy process throughout the PhD. Things become a lot less problem-free if the issues between you and your supervisor(s) are much more personal. These types of issues, if they arise, arise much later in the PhD. Switching supervisors later in the PhD is much more difficult. This is something I'll discuss in Chapter 29.

First-Year PhD Review

I've given a lot of thought as to how best represent articles I've written for the blog here in this book. I want them to fit the story I'm outlining, but I'm also wary of editing text I've written years ago to make it fit my feelings and knowledge now. As a result, I've decided to not edit these reviews at all. So what you're reading here is going to be an exact copy of my first-year review, as I wrote it 3 years ago. Don't be surprised if my writing has slightly "evolved".

I promised to answer questions on the blog as well. And no question was as popular as my honest opinion in my first year of the PhD, as I am about to finish it. So, here I will describe my experience.

Before we start, I should outline some details. I am a PhD student at the Warwick Business School (WBS), doing a PhD in Business and Management, with a specialization in Behavioral Science. However, I receive funding from both the WBS and the Economic and Social Research Council (ESRC). Some funding schemes make changes to the baseline of the first year in the PhD. It did at least for me. As a result of being ESRC funded, I entered a 1+3 program, meaning my first year would be another master's degree, an MA in Social Science Research.

Now, this sounds like a big change, but it really isn't. The difference between an ESRC and an exclusively WBS-funded student is very little, as the latter still has to do courses as well. It is just these courses would not necessarily happen at the same location, with the same people that you entered the PhD with.

Coursework

So normally, you enter the courses provided by the Business School. In total, you'd have seven courses over the year and an upgrade in September, just before starting the second academic year. This upgrade is to show your development over the past year, what you have written so far and how well you fit your own research.

These seven courses will not fit your research specialization. No one mentions that you are going to be doing courses at a rather low level, outside of your own specialization. So let me tell you. The cohort hired in my year for the Behavioral Science specialization is all people with backgrounds in economics. We all have experience with using statistical analysis programs (R, Matlab, Python, Stata) and have been trained quantitatively. So it was quite surprising when a group like this was forced to take courses in qualitative methods, that we do not know and will not use. It of course caused a lot of grumbling and whining. In hindsight it wasn't too bad, is what most of them will admit now.

There were non-topic-specific courses as well, which you could choose in the second term. These courses called themselves research operations or other meaningless names, and it was just everyone discussing their PhD topic and getting help with writing up drafts for the upgrade. Those courses were not bad at all.

You had topic-specific courses as well, such as Entrepreneurship, in which the broad directions of studying entrepreneurship were outlined. I quite enjoyed that one.

As I was ESRC, I had a slightly different course setup. I had six courses, of which four were ESRC taught and two had to be taken at the WBS. I ended up taking both Entrepreneurship and Theories of Organisation and Work, which are both very different from what I research. I thought it'd be funny to still branch out in my PhD. These courses were fine. I really did enjoy Entrepreneurship because so much of it is behavioral science applied to business.

The ESRC courses were similar to the mandatory WBS ones: quantitative methods, qualitative methods, philosophy of social science and research design and ethics. I will link the ESRC page if you'd like to read up on the program specifics.

Did I enjoy these courses? No. Was it the most awful thing I have ever done? No. Did I learn anything? Definitely not anything useful for my

PhD. But I got to hang out with people I wouldn't normally hang out with. And maybe I should explain why that is.

Interdisciplinarity

There is a reason such a wide variety of courses is being taught: the PhD students in the business school are not from the same disciplines. The WBS has several subgroups. One of them is Behavioral Science, there is Entrepreneurship and Innovation, there is Management Research, Finance and then some. As a result, there are people from quite different backgrounds. This makes working together very interesting. Especially when sharing an office. You start out being in an office with another 15 people. It helps bonding they say.

In the ESRC group, these differences were even more prominent. As people were in fact studying history and philosophy and were in the same class as psychology and business students. That truly was very eclectic. But mainly it was just hectic. In the courses that were being taught, especially quantitative methods, the differences in training slowed down the course to such an extent that it wasn't worth being taught. I am all for interdisciplinarity, but it does have to serve a purpose, not detract from it.

I will be honest in admitting that I took the ESRC funding offer because it is associated with a certain level of prestige. But their 1+3 is just a mess. If it weren't for the WBS Doctoral Program Office (DPO), which is not ESRC affiliated at all, I wouldn't have made it administratively. And that is something I want to very clearly state: having more than one funding source, knowing that they both have different guidelines and expectations can prove difficult. Not all programs are this bad. Leverhulme (Bridges) is great. So is Chancellors. But these programs don't add as many restrictions. I would recommend watching out for that.

Socializing

The other issue resulting from the ESRC's interdisciplinarity is that there is very little common ground between people. Moreover, there was no specific place to hang out together. As a result, hanging out with ESRC folks did not happen. This was also due to the fact that many ESRC students already had families, did not live close to campus, or had jobs next to the PhD as well. It was an odd mix of people.

In the WBS, it was much easier to get to know each other, as we shared a massive office. Especially if you did courses together. I don't go to the office myself much because I prefer working at home at all hours of the day, but I genuinely would recommend anyone to go. It's good to leave the house as a PhD student…

The reason I am emphasizing the social aspect is because doing a PhD can be very isolating. There is no genuine structure to it. You just have to meet your supervisors often enough and progress in your courses and research. It doesn't matter how, when, where and with whom you do this. As a result, you could go weeks without seeing anyone if you just want to work at home. This isolationism is why a lot of PhD students struggle with mental health issues such as anxiety and depression. So, going to the office is a good start to be surrounded by people. Get to know each other better and plan some things together. Have a movie night with a bunch of people from the office and grab a meal or a pint together. Before you know it, you are actually friends. I can genuinely promise it helps to just go out to the office.

Research

Supervisors are aware that due to the fact that you have courses, you will have limited time to spend on your own research. However, it is not like the workload of the course is that heavy, so it isn't an excuse to do nothing. Moreover, most people have in fact run at least one study or started working on a data set. This only affects quantitative students; those using qualitative methods have a different progression rate due to the intensity of their method.

Once the courses are over, students start to intensify the time allotted to writing up their literature review and outlining in detail the methodology that will be used in the research done in the upcoming 3 years. This is what will be presented at the upgrade.

On the ESRC 1+3, however, you will have to write a dissertation on top of doing your courses. Luckily, I had done a study myself in the first year. My research was in a real-life applied survey about the effect of payment methods on expenditure and expenditure recall. I was able to run this at the end of November with the help of my research assistants. As a result, I could repurpose the data and create a different research question to answer. I wrote 15,000 words about my new research question, using the already collected data from my first study, and will hand that in as my dissertation. It wasn't too much additional work.

Having run the study, even with help, during my coursework was intense. It was a lot of work and I have easily made 15-hour days to make sure it did actually work. But personally, I thought it was great to be able to run a study so quickly. So I was tired but over the moon.

Overall, I have had a very positive experience. Got on with my research. Supervisors and I are going strong, delving into the topic. Met some great people in the PhD itself to hang out with for the next 3 years. Been to some meetings and conferences, meeting more great people on professional and personal levels. I am very happy with my first year as a PhD student.

On the downside, the mandatory courses in the first year are not ideal, especially not the ESRC ones. I really don't think teaching data scientists at the PhD level how to do qualitative interviews is useful. But hey. Would it be enough reason to not do a PhD? It wouldn't for me. I can now just put another master title on my CV, which you can't do if you are just with the WBS, sorry guys.

And now I can continue to do my own research. For which I am very excited!

Concluding Remarks

A good start is half the work. Or at least, it'll be very helpful! Starting the PhD with the right expectations and laying the foundations for what will hopefully be a great step up in your career is key.

Whether you're staying at your alma mater or you're moving cities or even continents, there will be change. You'll be transitioning from exclusively doing coursework to (independent) research; you might be at a new institution or even in a new country. Regardless of the level of novelty, make the most of it. Give yourself time to explore your (new) surroundings and get to know the area, the locals and your colleagues. This is how you build a social life and a support network. And both of those things will keep you sane during the sometimes insane ride that is a PhD.

Do not skimp out on coursework either. It may be boring and you may be over it, but it needs to get done. And you may as well make the most of getting it done. If possible, choose courses that can level up your skillset. If that's not an option, tough it out and keep in mind that in the grand scheme of things doing some additional coursework is really a negligible amount of time and effort.

Despite coursework being important, the taught part of your PhD will not focus exclusively on the taught courses. You'll need to continue to focus on the PhD research itself, especially its planning. Talk with your supervisor(s) until you're both on the same page in terms of expectations, deadlines, schedules, work division and outcomes. What needs to get done when? Are there things you need to be looking out for? Are there possible delays such as ethics and finance applications? Were you aware of these? Was your supervisor aware of these?

In general, it's best to start talking to your supervisor(s) as soon as you can. Find out more about them, their workstyle, communication style and perception of you as a PhD student. It's important to know who you're dealing with and how they like to be dealt with.

It's not just your supervisor who you need to figure out, you'll need to figure out yourself too. Continue to ask yourself: what do you want from the PhD? You probably had a pretty solid idea when applying. Now, after several conversations with your supervisor(s) and colleagues, plus having now spent a short time in the PhD, is that idea still the same? Did you have to make some adjustments? Do you still feel good about the journey?

If for some reason you have lost a lot of excitement or enthusiasm, do check with yourself why that is. Did you come in with the wrong expectations? Are you struggling to communicate or connect with your supervisor? Is it just the coursework and lack of research getting you down?

Whatever it may be, it's important you constantly check with yourself how you're feeling about yourself, your work and the PhD as a whole. It's important to have this type of introspective insight early on. Because you're going to need it throughout the rest of your PhD. Which brings us to the next section!

Section 4

Getting on with the PhD!

Ok, so we're back here again. You've progressed to yet another stage. Contemplation, application and initiation. All of those three stages can be crossed off your bucket list. Now, we get to the real chunk of the PhD, where the real action is.

As things stand, a lot of the issues mentioned in this part of the book might have already popped up a lot earlier. Maybe you've already considered tacking on additional collaborators beyond your supervisory unit. Maybe this is common in your research group, maybe it isn't.

On the same track, maybe you've known about maintaining your mental health for a long time already and I'm offering no new tips here. Very much in line with this, maybe the shift from going from a very structured working environment to a non-structured environment is something you've experienced before. Maybe it's even something that you're welcoming with open arms. Who knows?

What I'm trying to say is, we're all different. This section is a bit of a collection of things that I've struggled with, that colleagues of mine have struggled with or that are part of a larger debate regarding academia (especially Twitter is very active in this domain). If you are in a PhD program currently or have finished one already, you might identify with these problems, or you might not identify with them at all. If you are considering doing a PhD or have only just started, use this section of the book as a guideline to identifying and dealing with common problems when doing a PhD. It already helps loads if you can recognize a problem as is.

One key message I want to really emphasize: just because your problem isn't in this section doesn't mean it doesn't exist. I'm not claiming that the list of topics discussed is an exhaustive list, it really isn't. And trust me when I tell you, when you're facing a problem within the PhD, you're not alone. There are lots of great resources online that can help you with this. Just post a question on Twitter using the #AcademicTwitter or #PhD and see how many replies, messages and retweets you get. These tags manage to reach hundreds if not thousands who are, or have been, in a similar position and can offer advice.

With all that out of the way, let's dive into some things to consider when fully settled into the PhD!

Structure Amidst Chaos

Whether you micromanage every minute of your own day or whether you feel like time is more of a social construct, by this stage in your PhD, with your coursework obligations gone, you must have noticed a slight shift. This shift is rather obvious: your time has (sort of) become your own. The idea of deadlines has essentially faded to the background as they are now on a horizon which spans years rather than weeks.

Some people love this. Not having to get up at a certain time each morning or not having an entire week planned out is what gets them going. And if that's you, fair play to you, just make sure you do actually make the big deadline at the end of your PhD. You know, actually submitting the bugger.

Some people, myself included, hate this. Being able to set your own working hours is nice, I'll admit to that. It worked miracles for me. But for some people, this turns into a never-ending battle of trying to motivate themselves to get to work, because it doesn't technically speaking have to happen now.

And others, probably the largest group, have no idea at the very start of their PhD whether being in charge over your own time is really what they want or not. And ironically enough, you won't figure out which style fits you best during the taught aspect of your PhD, because even then, with all the freedom you technically speaking might still have, there is a structure.

Most PhD trajectories are structureless. Of course, not all are. If your PhD is integrated within a company, such as a consultancy, manufacturer or medical research center, you're now simply on the company's structure. This may also hold for people who do a lot of lab work and people who signed up for a pre-structured PhD. The latter often has a grant which is very time-constrained and outlines very clearly what needs to happen when. So there is your structure!

Now, let's look at PhDs which are slightly more "free". There is the idea that you need to have x amount of publishable papers at the end of x number of years. Or you need to have an entire dissertation of x number of words/pages at the end of x number of years. As far as structure goes, that's not that rigid, is it? Some might even say it's rather free.

When I say free, I'm not saying there won't be any constraints placed on you. At the university business school where I was based, there were still upgrades (first to second year) and annual reviews (from the second year onwards). These were check-ins on a departmental level just to see if you'd progressed enough in that year to make it to the end properly. Meaning, being able to submit on time.

Again, this might not be enough structure for you still. And that's fair, one annual deadline didn't help me either. It's easy enough to figure out what you can do in a week. But what on earth can you achieve in an entire year? Would you plan it out per month, or per week? And would that be realistic? Most people don't tend to bet on this strategy to get them where they need to be. And that's fair.

Now, throughout the problem statement, you might have been wondering: what exactly is the issue here? Most people would kill to have a more flexible job, determine their own hours and be able to work from home if so desired (this has massively changed during the pandemic, which I think is actually a good development. Silver lining I suppose). But keep in mind that most things aren't what they're cracked up to be. And flexibility is definitely one of these things.

Of course, people can use flexibility to suit their own working hours. Maybe you're a morning and an evening person, and it's the afternoon that's just not productive (like me). Well, the PhD will give you the flexibility to work those hours without anyone complaining. Or, if you're just a morning person, well you can start at 5 am if you so desire. The same goes for an evening person, if you want to start at 5 pm, you do that. There's no one really who can tell you otherwise. As long as your work gets done.

So yes, flexibility can be great. I'm not saying it's by default a bad thing, because it isn't. It's just that a lot of people work better with some type of structure in place. And flexibility often doesn't provide that. When I said that flexibility was a great thing, *as long as your work gets done*, well, that's a big caveat.

What does flexibility look like when it backfires? Well, it can result in people working all hours of the day, or not working at all. In the former you might still get a lot of your work done, maybe you'll even get ahead of the curve. People around you will look at your progress and be impressed, and ask themselves "how do they do it?!" Well, you do it by continuously working. No breaks, no 9–5, no evenings off, no weekends and no holidays. If there's no one who tells you when to work, it's entirely possible you go way beyond crazy.

There might be several reasons why someone starts to work like this. The first is there genuinely being too much work. If there's literally never an end to the to-do list, that is rather odd. If that's the case, have a chat with your supervisors. Maybe you're not working smart enough, there might be easier ways of going about the tasks you're doing. Also, are you certain all of the work needs to be done *now*? Maybe your sense of urgency isn't grounded in reality. Someone who knows more about the PhD trajectory timewise, a.k.a. your supervisor or a more experienced colleague, can help you out with your planning or can help you create a realistic timeline. Sometimes stuff is actually just too much for one person and simply needs to be outsourced, and hopefully, it can be. Again, a conversation to have with your supervisor(s)!

Quick disclaimer: there will be weeks when a PhD, or any job really, can take this form or intensity. Especially towards the end or during a time-intensive part of a study there might be periods during which you'll have to work "abnormal" hours. It only becomes an issue when this turns into a constant. Where there's no time to recharge and this moves from being a "work" issue to being a mental and physical health issue. I'm drawing your attention to the possible effects of a structure, or lack thereof, so we can avoid that!

Moving onto the opposite: not working at all. Or working very limited hours. Actually, when push comes to shove, I can't say I deeply care about the hours you work. I didn't care too much about the hours I worked either. Let's put this differently: due to the lack of structure, you're not working long/hard/intensely enough to get your work done.

Some people thrive on the feeling of urgency. You know, the type that doesn't start a project until the week (or even day) it's due? The type of people who leave everything till the last minute because the pressure focuses them and doesn't allow for distractions? Well, I personally cannot relate, because I don't deal with that type of anxiety well, but this type of procrastination is really common. People who only really work (well) under stress and immediate looming deadlines are really common. But how does that work in a PhD where the deadline is several years away?

Again, you'll need to tell someone that whatever's going on isn't working, because, well, you aren't working. This isn't your supervisor's first time round the block. They should be aware of the different working styles that exist, and how to accommodate them. Very likely the solution is for them to set you artificial deadlines to get certain things done. "Have a study design ready by the end of the month" or "write up this chapter fully in 2 months' time and present it to us" are common ways of providing motivation and a sense of urgency to PhD students who need it.

So, how can we fix either underworking or overworking? Annual reviews aren't frequent enough to really direct work, for most people. But how about monthly or even more frequent meetings? The first point of contact as a PhD supervisee (which I'm assuming you are) is their supervisor(s). Going back to Chapter 18, you need to figure out how to "handle" your supervisor, as well as they need to figure out how to "handle" you. You are (a minimum of) two different people who are now trying to work together. As I've already mentioned, make clear what you expect and need of each other and take it from there. Now, I happened to meet both my supervisors, at the same time, on an almost weekly basis. This worked for us as I did have progress to report and issues that needed to be resolved on a weekly basis, so it made sense. If you don't have this, weekly meetings might not be necessary. Some supervisors are perfectly happy meeting multiple times a week during a busy period in your PhD, and if it's not a busy period, you can just not meet. All of that is perfectly valid. But if it's the lack of structure and deadlines you're struggling with, do indicate this to them, and do suggest that more frequent regular meetings might help you get yourself in order. Whatever works right?

Your supervisor should want to see you succeed, and to some extent (within limits), should want to accommodate your workstyle. If you require more frequent meetings to work well or to feel as if you're working well, that's really not too much to ask for, granted that these meetings are actually achieving that goal.

However, it is entirely within the realm of possibilities that your supervisor can't (or won't…) meet more frequently with you. This is why I strongly advise you to do your research with regard to potential supervisors. If they're world-renowned and work for both the university, several other initiatives and the UN, can you really be surprised if they can't make the time to meet you on a weekly basis? Exactly. This is why that stuff was important tens of chapters ago!

Anyway, onto the solution. If your supervisor cannot give you structure, who might be able to? Some people work within bigger (research) groups. See if there's someone else who can hold you accountable. An accountability buddy, if you will. Work together, discuss the research together and plan together. Make them your mentor if you can. Yes, your mentor can be a very different person from your supervisor. This was definitely true in my case, and honestly, it's fine. If the person you've picked as your accounta-buddy is on your own level, an actual colleague of yours who's in the same boat, they can be really helpful too, but keep in mind you're going to have to return the favor and help them out too! Later on in this section, we will also look into collaborating beyond your original supervisory unit, and this might pose a great solution as well!

So yes, flexibility doesn't work for everyone, and if you're struggling with it, I hope that some of the initial solutions are able to help you out. Honest and open conversations with your supervisors about what is and isn't working for you are always a good idea. I'd always use this as a first step. From thereon, there are several other steps you can take as outlined above.

And here's another insider secret: no one is going to raise an eyebrow when you decide to work your PhD as a 9–5 job. If that works for you, then you should do exactly that.

Teaching

If you're someone who struggles with work when there's little to no structure and prefers to have some sort of structure, well, teaching might be for you!

It might be a slightly odd way of motivating someone to go into teaching, but it does work. Obviously, it would be better if your motivation for starting teaching was the fact that you genuinely want to communicate information to younger generations for the betterment of society. But before we even start diving into the motivations for teaching, a first question should probably be: does your PhD require you to teach?

Some PhD programs and contracts have clearly outlined that the PhD student needs to teach a certain number of hours or courses. Often the courses to be taught in that case are also those of the supervisor, as a way of helping them out. The latter is not always the case but often is. Again, discuss this with your supervisor. If it's the case that you need to teach during your contract, we don't need to discuss your motivation, you'll just have to do it!

Even if the contract itself doesn't specify it, some, if not most, prospective academic jobs, such as post-docs and assistant professorships, will require you to have taught before. So, even if it's not a direct requirement of the PhD, it might be a direct requirement for the jobs you're aiming for after the PhD. So again, your motivation doesn't matter, you need to have teaching experience.

Now, I have a feeling I'm not really "selling" teaching as an experience but more as a mandate, but it's actually both. I personally really enjoyed teaching, it wasn't mandatory for me to do so, and I'm no longer aiming for jobs for which it would be a requirement, so technically speaking, I never really had to teach. But then it also has to be mentioned: a lot of people enjoy teaching, and not a lot of PhD students get away with not teaching at all.

Two reasons for the latter: your department will want you to contribute, and it's odd to not have teaching experience as part of your PhD, given that teaching is part of academia. Looking into the first, you'll roll into an everlasting debate on how most institutions clearly put the emphasis on research and not on teaching; there never being enough resources allocated to teaching; and PhD students being used as cheap labor. Now, I won't get into this debate, although I do think there are valid concerns being raised. However, for you as a PhD student, partaking in this debate is not going to change how you need to do your PhD or at least the teaching part of it. So, good luck teaching!

Another argument for teaching in your PhD: it pays. Most PhD contracts will have a teaching obligation, but that obligation will be compensated (I have seen PhD contracts in which teaching is obligatory and non-compensated. Read the small print!). I have outlined the financial pressures and the opportunity cost of a PhD in Section 1, and I stand by those. If you can't afford to do a PhD, don't do one. However, the financial pressure that you may experience can be relieved by teaching. It (often) does bring in money.

I'm not saying teaching is going to make you rich, because it won't. But it can help. On that level, you should definitely consider it.

Now I've painted a list of reasons to teach, but none of them are very intrinsic. I simply outlined that often teaching is mandatory, in different forms, and that for some there'll also be financial incentives for teaching. There'll also be people who genuinely love teaching, and want to have more experience doing it. And last but not least, there'll be people who will use teaching as a way of imposing structure onto their PhDs and motivating themselves to work. Whichever type of person you are, let's look into some aspects of teaching that you should be aware of.

First, it can take up a lot of time. If you're lucky, you'll be a seminar tutor who "just" has to go through the slides which also exist, made by the previous tutors or even the module leader, and explain several concepts to undergraduates. If you're even luckier, this module is in your field of expertise and doesn't require you to do any real preparation, because you already know what's going on. If you're not so lucky, the slides still need to be made, parts of the module still need to be structured, materials need to be reviewed and it's not in your field of expertise, or even in your field. This will obviously will require quite a lot of preparation on your part. Often, you will get paid for preparation time as well, either explicitly (you have specific hours of pay for this) or implicitly (the hourly wage assumes preparation and is high(er) as a result of it). To explain implicit and explicit pay a bit better, I happen to know the PhD teaching rates for two universities, at least for their business school and economics department respectively. One pays around 16 pounds per hour, but gives you hours for preparing, teaching, office hours, marking and "other" (that can be anything, but is often for training purposes). The other institution pays about 60 pounds per hour *taught* but assumes that 1 hour of teaching requires several hours of preparation and office hours. I'm pretty sure marking is still paid separately. That's really the difference you should be aware of.

Anyway, back to time allocation: it differs a lot per course how much time is required to get a seminar up and running, and what the financial compensation is for that work. Given that you sign up for TA'ing (teaching assistance) well in advance, you do need to figure out with both your own planning and that of your supervisors whether you'll have enough time to teach in certain periods of your PhD. If there are periods you need to be in the lab 9–5 or even longer, well, that doesn't lend itself to teaching very well. However, if your PhD is more flexible, or you have a period within your PhD that'll be more flexible, maybe use that as a time to experience teaching.

Second, you're not likely to be a natural. Sorry. There are quite a few people I know who are good teachers. There's even a handful whom I would consider to be excellent teachers. But most of them only got to that level of quality because they teach. A lot. And they enjoy teaching.

When you start out teaching, TA'ing and leading seminars, unless you have a personality which somehow makes you a natural teacher or you somehow had a buck load of experience already, you're not going to be that great at it. Luckily, most universities and their respective departments do offer teaching training, and I suggest you take it. Although it's likely to be mandatory anyway.

I can hardly prepare you for that training nor can I really explain to you how to teach. It goes both beyond the scope of this book, and way beyond me as a person. One tip I can give you: remember the best teachers you had and ask yourself: why did you think they were so great? I think that'll be a good starting point to figure out what kind of teacher you'd want to be.

Another aspect of teaching and the type of teaching you'll be doing has only come up recently. Recently meaning in the past 2 years. I'm obviously talking about the side effects of the pandemic and having to move things online. Massive Online Open Courses (MOOCs) have become incredibly popular throughout, but most university courses were still taught on-site and offline. However, the pandemic has shifted most if not all teaching (if possible) to the online environment and that might feel a bit strange at the start. It can be very odd, quite daunting or just plain annoying to have to talk to your own computer for several hours on end, to people who mostly have their cameras off and do not seem to interact much. Which brings me very nicely to the next point.

Third, not all aspects of teaching are enjoyable. Even if you love teaching, you won't love all of teaching. There are just certain aspects of teaching that aren't as great as others. For example, whether online or offline, getting a discussion on a topic going with students who are both well prepared, well versed and very engaged is amazing. On the other hand, standing in front of a class that has clearly not prepared for the seminar, awkward silences and no interaction are not so amazing. Both scenarios can happen.

It's also entirely possible that you love interacting with students, but hate marking. Marking is not a very entertaining part of teaching, but it is a necessity. Bad things happen. I just need you to be wary of the fact that there'll be drawbacks to teaching, as well as there being benefits.

All in all, I really enjoyed teaching. It led to some nice discussions, it got me more acquainted with certain subdomains in my field and it did give me a nice financial kickback. Ultimately, teaching helped me grow as a teacher, a person and as an academic. What more could you want?

Conferences

Another exciting part of the PhD, or academia in general, is the conferences. You get to travel (depending on the circumstances), meet new people (network), find out what's new in your field and maybe even get to present your own work. Awesome! But how do you go about it?

Finding conferences

The first thing I want to talk about is finding conferences. Your first point of contact here are your supervisors (again) and other people in the research group you work with or are vaguely related to in a collegial way. What conferences do they go to? Which conferences have they been to? Which conferences do they recommend for you, both with regard to your research and you being an early career researcher? I think that in and of itself should give you a comprehensive list.

Second step is to have a look online. Surprise. You can just look for your topic of study or the name of your (sub)field and the word conference as the next keyword and you should find a wealth of information. The conferences already recommended to you should show up, as well as maybe some additional conferences. Make sure you read their site carefully and decide whether this is the conference for you.

When having made a list of conferences that you're interested in, make sure to write down their dates somewhere. These dates are both the date that the conference is actually happening as well as the dates for abstract/paper submission if you want to be a speaker, as well as the date for buying your conference ticket. Those are likely separate dates, so keep them somewhere!

Attending conferences

As already mentioned above, you can go to a conference as an attendee or a speaker. These are two different things.

When attending a conference you're just a guest. You listen to other people present and are allowed to ask clarifying questions during the presentation, but that is essentially it. After the presentations and during the network sessions or discussion panels, you might be able to get more of a word in about your own work, but that's not as easy as it seems.

When you attend a conference as a speaker, you fulfill both roles, if you want to. Obviously, you'll have to present your work, for which you'll receive questions from the audience. You might also take part in a discussion group or panel; it depends on what type of speaking you've been invited to or allocated to. You'll know this well in advance so there shouldn't be any surprises there. As a speaker, it's likely that people will come to you during network and discussion rounds. However, you can also still be a guest yourself and approach others. One doesn't exclude the other.

For PhD students, there is an obvious advantage to attending as a speaker: you get to present your work and get feedback on it from those in your field. This feedback will be highly critical but is often very useful for determining the next steps in your research. I would most definitely recommend it.

From the PhD student perspective, there is another more administrative part of conferences to keep in mind: finance. Most conferences will require at least a conference fee (ticket price) which can easily rack up to over $100. Most conferences will also not be around the corner and might require travel (assuming they're not online, for obvious reasons), which is also not free. Going to a conference can be a rather expensive pursuit.

Now, where is this money going to come from? Well, most PhD programs include a conference allowance. It really depends on your program, contract, department and funder(s) how this allowance works, but someone somewhere should refund you the money. As I said, this allowance can take many different shapes and forms. Some PhD programs have a specific pot of money to allocate to attending conferences per year and that money cannot be carried over into the next year. Sometimes, it can be carried over. Some programs have a general allowance for PhD students from which they have to pay for conferences, research costs, training and other things required. It's so diverse that it's really difficult to make any generalizable statements about it. My advice: check with your funder, they ought to have a system in place or that. And if they don't, check with your department and next with your supervisor(s). The money has to come from somewhere, and it better not be your pocket.

Presenting

As you progress through your PhD, it's increasingly more likely that you're a presenter rather than "just" a guest. You'll have more work to talk about, and you'll have gotten over the initial fright that your research isn't as good as that of others who've been "in the buzz" a lot longer. Now, let me give you some tips on presenting at a conference.

It is important to check in advance how big, but mainly how formal a conference is. Especially if you are presenting, you don't want to be in front of hundreds of people in suits, when you are wearing jeans and sneakers (although a friend of mine once attended a formal conference where one of the presenters was a well-respected academic in a gold and black Adidas tracksuit. He will not soon be forgotten).

Other things you might want to keep in mind besides your own looks are the looks of your presentation. I'm afraid that most of what people perceive are peripheral cues and not content cues, so make sure your PowerPoint (or Latex, whatever you use) has "suited up" as well. Try to avoid endless sentences and text, break things up with (relevant!) pictures and just in general, watch your own pace. Stopping for emphasis is a great idea. Stopping to just take a breathing break can help too. It gives you time to, well, breathe and for the audience to catch up and take a mental breath. This ensures that the little content they do take in is being taken in properly. On the topic of taking breaks, are you taking questions during your presentation, or only after? If you are a person that easily has their "flow" disrupted, you might want to opt for the latter. Do make this clear at the beginning of your presentation though and do make sure you've accounted for these breaks in your presentation duration. Most conferences give you a maximum number of minutes to present. Stick with those!

Now you've just finished presenting. Good job. But at a conference, your session doesn't end when you finish presenting. Now the time has come for comments, suggestions and questions. Sometimes, this part of the presentation can be longer and much more nerve-wrecking than the actual presentation. Stay calm and allow yourself to think before replying. This ensures you don't have extremely emotional responses where you are trying to defend your research, rather than listening and analyzing the information given to you. People at conferences, especially when in your own field of study, tend to know *what's up*. So stay calm, ask for clarification when needed, reply in a neutral tone and write down suggestions and recommendations. When you are writing down suggestions or recommendations, this makes you seem interested and eager to learn/improve, but in general it signals you are open to critique and communication. It will make you much more respected within the community.

As I've said before, there'll be a time limit on your presentation, which also extends to the question and suggestion round. If there was someone you still wanted to talk to about their question or suggestion, make sure to reach out to them during one of the discussion or networking breaks. Or just after the conference itself via email.

Networking

Going to conferences is a great way of staying up to date with your field and getting feedback on your own work, but it's also a great way to get to know the people in your field better. Maybe you can establish a collaboration. Maybe you can find yourself a way into working in their research group. Maybe you're setting up connections to ease into your next job. It's all known as networking.

Successful networking is networking in which you are actually aware of who the other person is, what they do, what they're interested in doing and how you can help them with the latter. This is the type of networking where you're essentially talking yourself into a job. Networking can also be just talking to people who are doing similar work to you, without much of an agenda. As I mentioned in the "presenting" section, you can just walk up to someone and ask them more about the comments they made about your presentation. Or, if they were the presenter, you can just walk up to them and talk more about their presentation. Networking can be rather free-flowing.

If you feel like you weren't able to talk to someone during the conference itself, due to time constraints or for other reasons, you can always reach out to them via email, just as you would if you wanted more feedback from someone on your own presentation. Email is a bit tricky as a lot of people receive a lot of emails so you might have to send the same email several times, but in the end, I'm sure they'll reply. In the email itself, you can ask if they have time to set up a 30-minute call to discuss their or your or both your work more and whether collaboration is possible.

Networking can also be very planned, rather than free-flowing. During an interview for the Questioning Behaviour Podcast, one of the early career researchers gave us a great tip: if she was attending a conference where there was a speaker she really wanted to talk to, she'd reach out to the speaker well in advance, telling them that they would be at the same conference and whether they'd be happy to meet up with her before the conference day would start for a cup of coffee and a quick chat. I thought it was pretty ballsy, but it sure as hell sounds effective. She had a 100% success rate with that tactic!

Now, I know that networking isn't for everyone. Some people love it, some hate it. But just think of it as a way of trying to find out "who's who" in your field, and letting them get to know you. Whether you like it or not, this type of exposure is actually really important.

I've always really enjoyed going to conferences. When they started moving online, it was quite a switch, but as time progressed, the online format has started to work really well. I personally really enjoy presenting my own work or discussing behavioral science and the developments in the field in general. In addition, coming back to structure and time management, having to present at a conference is a clear deadline for having your work in order. So there's that!

Writing It All Down

Now on top of doing teaching, your actual research, attending conferences and maybe even presenting at conferences, you're going to have to write. That thesis isn't writing itself.

A lot of people seem to struggle with the actual writing part of the PhD. Writing, however, is rather a crucial part of doing a PhD, and doing research in general. There'll be no thesis without writing, even if your thesis is the most practical, the most applied or just the most contained project ever. There will be words. There will be chapters.

What you're supposed to write and how you're supposed to write it depends on your field, PhD structure, institution and maybe even cohort. Some PhD theses are entire stories, beautifully written out from beginning to end and almost read like a book. This is more likely in the humanities. In the sciences, you tend to have a more rigid format with an introduction, review of prior work, your experiments (methods, results), a large discussion section placing the results into the context of prior work, and if you're fancy (or need to hit a certain word limit) a conclusion. The social sciences tend to fall somewhere in between, where both options may be available to you.

Due to the scope of possibilities, here I have but one piece of advice: make sure you check with your supervisor(s) or your department what your options are in terms of format. If you have options, discuss with your supervisor(s) what the best fit may be for your work. If you don't have options and there is a single format, well, you now know what to aim for.

Having established the format you can write accordingly. In Chapter 16, I outlined the importance of planning your research, even during the taught parts of your PhD. This planning also included diving back into the literature, as this would let you establish what work had already been done, and how it had been done, so you would know which topics to avoid, to dive deeper into and which methodology to apply to do so.

Now, it would have been "oh so convenient" had you summarized these articles as you went through them. You'd have done this partially for your research proposal and will have to do it again for your PhD thesis, but in much more detail, displaying a higher level of writing. So, I recommend that every article you read on your PhD topic gets saved, highlighted and summarized, granted that it was useful to your research.

The writing up of the literature review, or the prior work review section, or whichever name this section or chapter may have for your PhD thesis, can be done at any point in time. In the case of my PhD specifically, it was required to have a draft of the full literature review at the end of the very first year of the PhD. Personally, I thought that this was very useful. Not only does it set a deadline and gives you some structure (Chapter 20, if you're struggling with structure), but it really forced me to dive deeper into the literature. It also helps if your supervisors have something to look at to see if you haven't missed any work and help you edit your writing to get it to the next level.

Most institutions will have deadlines for seeing the introduction or literature review, so you will have to write it out anyway! And once you have, I really do recommend sending it to your supervisor(s) to get them to check it.

In terms of writing out your actual research, meaning your own work, it becomes a bit trickier. No institution I'm aware of has deadlines indicating that *the result section of study 3 of Chapter 5* should be finished by December of your fourth year of the PhD. That would be insane and useless. What isn't insane, nor useless, is for you to start planning your research writing at the same time as you're planning the research itself.

Regardless of what your research actually entails, once you've established the idea, your supervisor(s) have signed off on it, the study has been designed, the materials obtained, the participants recruited, the medicine created or the machine built (I'm trying to reach all fields here), you are moving onto conducting the research. There is now a clear timeline for when you are conducting the research, and when you are not, and no longer will be. So, if we know all of this, we can also plan the writing.

There are two timeframes of "not conducting research": you are in the middle of the research, but for some reason are currently not conducting it, or you have actually finished all of your research. The former can be caused by all types of things: (1) your participant didn't turn up, (2) something isn't working the way it should, or at all, delaying the research, (3) you only do research in the mornings to leave your afternoons open for other work, or (4) any other reason really. Regardless of the reason, you do actually have time available. Maybe you should use that time to write?

A lot of people seem to think you're best off conducting all of the research first, doing the analysis, knowing your results and then writing up your research in one go. There is an argument to be made for that, definitely. But how does that work if you have multiple projects running at the same time? And if because of this structure, you never find the time to write because you're constantly conducting research?

This is where I see a lot of people struggle. Because they are still conducting the research, they keep pushing the actual writing up of the research further and further ahead. But this doesn't work. If your entire PhD thesis is a single project, e.g. an ethnographic study, writing everything up in the end may work, as you are working with a single topic. Although I still highly doubt whether this would be an effective strategy as you will be dealing with a multitude of themes and subthemes, which will require high-level structural writing to translate properly. If your PhD thesis consists of multiple projects, how well do you believe you can keep them apart to neatly write them up in the end? I don't think you can.

My advice is as follows: for each and every project, write up a literature review section as soon as you've established the main idea of the project, this should also motivate your hypotheses or research questions. Write up the methodology section as soon as you have conceptualized it and lock it in (pre-registration is more common in some fields than in others). Write up the result section as soon as you have analyzed the results and both you and your supervisor(s) have agreed on how to write them down to make a cohesive (enough) story. Send this version of events to your supervisor(s) and see what they say. Them going through your written work will take a while and will likely also require a lot of edits. There may be versions

1 through 12 at the end of this process, but what you're left with will be good. After having established this version, it's time to add in the discussion, to place the results into context and refer back to earlier work. Last, you write an introduction to your project, and if required a conclusion. Ironically, both are supposed to summarize what happened in the research. And there you have it. Now send it back to the supervisors until it is *polished*.

This sounds like a very structured and organized process. It can be, but it often isn't. I remember talking to a postdoctoral researcher who had a PhD supervisor who always wrote the first paper together with them, so they had that foundation. I thought that that was amazing, and I'd suggest that anyone try this with their supervisor. Worst they could say is no, right?

Why is this often not such a structured and organized process? Well, because people aren't structured and organized either. And neither is research. As soon as you have results that are counterintuitive, difficult to explain, or just odd, this neat structure goes out the window. Your supervisor(s) and you, or your supervisors among themselves, may not agree on the story to tell, may not agree on the literature to reference or the conclusions to draw from the results. This sets back progress by several weeks if not more. It's because things like this happen and everything always takes much longer than expected, that I recommend writing constantly because I find that leaving it till the end is a terrible alternative. Because the end is always so much closer than you thought it'd be.

There is an issue that warrants addressing in terms of writing: in the earlier paragraphs, I keep referring to writing up a project or writing up your research. But you don't really write those up willy-nilly. There are formats for that. So next question: are we writing papers, or are we writing chapters? Because these are not the same thing.

Writing a chapter is directly writing for your PhD thesis. A chapter is part of the bookwork that is your thesis. As I've said before, how you should write up your thesis, and therefore your chapters, depends on your institution. They might require that the thesis is split a certain way, with separate chapters for the introduction, literature review, study 1, study 2, …, study n, discussion and conclusion. The chapters on study 1 until study n are likely to only be the motivation, methodology and results for that particular study. Your entire PhD could also only be a single, much larger study, in which case that chapter is much bigger, and potentially the lion's share of the thesis. Again, that completely depends on your field and institution. The main thing here is, a chapter needs to fit the standards of the institution. So does the thesis overall, which will very likely have a minimum and maximum in terms of word limit, page limit, etc. At most institutions, the standard of a chapter is that it needs to be of "publishable quality".

Writing a paper is different in that its standards are defined by the journal you are submitting it to. They determine word limit, page limit, paper structure (sections to include, or not include), where the images go, whether you're allowed an appendix and what goes into the appendix, etc. Obviously, if you submit the work to a journal, it should be of publishable quality, otherwise it's a sure rejection. Another key difference here is that if one journal rejects you and you want to submit the paper to another journal, you'll probably have to do large rewrites on it, to fit the standards of the second journal, as it may have entirely different standards as to what a manuscript should look like. Some journals have specific word limits on certain sections (e.g. the introduction and discussion cannot exceed 1,000 words), and others don't. The ones that don't will often want to see much larger sections outlining the motivation and contribution of the paper. Because of these differences, some students and also higher-level academics (all the way to the professor level) choose to have a "base" version of the paper, which may look a lot like a chapter. This base version will have all the information, which can then be copied over and fitted to the journal requirements, never editing the actual base version. Whether you'll want to work with such a base version is obviously your own choice, but given that your thesis will require chapters which are essentially these base versions, it does make sense!

Also, don't think for a second that writing chapters and/or papers is the only writing you'll be doing in either the PhD or any academic career. Forget it. Throughout the book, so far you've read references to research proposals, grant proposals, ethics applications, research or additional funding applications, conference applications, presentations, upgrades (or other progression documents) and pre-registrations. And don't forget the many emails you'll be writing!

All jokes aside, you're going to have to get to writing, and I really don't recommend leaving it until the end. I really don't think you'll have the time and mental capacity left at the very end of the PhD to do the very best job of it. I think one massive drawback of writing it all up at the end is the lack of time you give yourself but also the lack of time you give your supervisor(s) or whoever is reading and editing your work. I have learned so much, and my academic writing has improved so much by having my supervisors go over it again and again. Sure, it is really demotivating to get back version 37 covered in red text and comments (the way my supervisor edits) and having to go over it. Again. But it does improve your writing. And the next paper (or chapter) you write will be better as a result of this. So don't short-change yourself out of this learning process. Make sure you start writing things down early. And make sure you send those things out to your supervisors. Don't be nervous or anxious for critiques, that's part of the learning process. Send it to colleagues or friends first if you're really nervous about your supervisors reading it. But make sure you get stuff on paper and that it gets to your supervisor(s) within a manageable time-frame. As my supervisor always said: you can't edit a blank page.

For those who really struggle to get to writing, every university has writing initiatives, where people get together (also virtually) to motivate each other to write. The one at my university was called "Write here, write now", which I thought was quite cute. I know Academic Twitter has the "100 days of writing" initiative as well. And I'm sure there are many more I'm just not aware of.

You need to plan hours or days or maybe even weeks of writing into the PhD schedule, it's an absolute must. And if you're struggling with planning, refer back to Chapter 20 on structure, or skip to Chapter 25 to read more about time management in general.

The Publication Journey

In the previous chapter, I've described the importance of writing. Obviously, a massive goal of the PhD is to get your research and your written chapters into paper format and then submit them to a journal. I think the "publication journey" is one of the most elusive journeys in academia. Which is odd, because that journey leads to the goal which is most desired and by which your entire worth as an academic seems to be determined. I think it would do us all some good if I broke this process down for you.

Now obviously, there is a lot of work that comes *before* the actual submission to a journal. I may not have gone into all the details equally, but by now you should have gathered that your work, your research, will involve literature reviews, summarizing prior work, ideation, research questions, further literature review, methodology design (possible pre-registration), financial and ethical applications, hopefully some writing (see Chapter 23), possible product or experiment building and that is before we even conduct any research in the first place!

Next, we conduct the research. Hopefully, all goes well. It may not go well. Adjustments may need to be made. Re-hypothesize, re-design and re-conduct. Results?! Are the results any good? Do they fit with prior work or not? Should they? Do they need to? Is further analysis required, if so, unfortunately, rinse and repeat. I have to add, by the way, that this isn't typical of a PhD. This is typical of research. So keep that in mind. More analysis. Satisfied with the results? More writing. Discussion. Determine context. What is the story here? Is there a better, more convincing story?

Do we need more data for that? Can we get more data for that? Etc., etc. It's a long process, and the write-up isn't finished yet.

Writing it up the final version then. Have we agreed on a story? Great! Have your supervisors checked the initial draft yet? Not yet… Oh wait they have. They don't agree on the story. More discussions. Good grief…

This is a process, and it's one hell of a process before the word journal even gets mentioned. As discussed in Chapter 23, if you want to publish in a journal, you need to select a journal and follow its standard and requirements for a manuscript. Some people write up without a journal in mind, they have a general "base" version of the entire paper. Then, they select a journal and a category of paper within that journal (some journals have long and short-form papers or fast-track publication routes with different requirements). They then adapt the paper to fit the criteria of that journal and its style. Others don't have a general version; they select a journal and then write around these criteria; they do not write beforehand. The latter might seem quicker, but there are advantages to having a base version to go from, such as not constantly having to do a full rewrite but being able to copy-paste and edit from the base. This helps especially if the initial journal had a short-form paper style and the next journal now has a long form. Which style you choose depends entirely on yourself. And possibly your supervisor(s).

One version of the paper is finished. Excellent! I would recommend you take a moment to appreciate how far you have come. Now, the paper as it is should be in the right shape to submit to a journal. So let's do that.

Going into a journal submission portal, you need about 200 different university accounts, but once you're in, you're in! Upload your documents, making sure you stick with the criteria, fill in all your details (and those of co-authors) and select your reviewers and editors. Oh yeah, did I not mention that before? Another discussion to have with your supervisors: who do they know in this topic? This step requires a lot of researching and soul-searching, but once you know who to select you should be good. Select, upload cover letter (not necessary for each journal) and submit. Fantastic!

Now you wait. About 75%, if not more, of the papers get desk rejected. This means that the main editor looks at it, finds fault with it and lets you know within approximately 2 weeks that the paper is not up to the standards of the journal. The remaining 25% (or so) goes to round 2, where they are reviewed by the other editors. They decide whether the paper will be sent to the reviewers. Again, the majority does not make the cut. This process takes over another month, easily. Then, if you are one of the lucky few, your paper will be reviewed by your selected reviewers, which can take another several months. And then, after months and months of waiting, you can still be rejected.

However, rejection is not the only option here. You can also receive conditional acceptance or a revise and resubmit (r&r). These are essentially on the same spectrum, where conditional acceptance often indicates minor edits and the r&r requires more major edits. The rejection is the final end of the spectrum which requires such major edits that the journal (or at least the reviewers your paper dealt with) deem it unpublishable.

What are you supposed to do when you receive either of these outcomes? The lucky thing is that it's the reviewers' job to tell you. Once the result is in the journal editor will send you a letter summarizing their take on the reviewers' opinions, give their own opinion and include the exact comments of the reviewers on what the paper further requires to be accepted for publication. With a conditional acceptance, the reviewers will have listed the minor edits that need doing. You simply do these minor edits and resubmit the paper as is outlined in the letter sent by the editor. This shouldn't take you too long at all. Once you resubmit and the editor approves of the new manuscript, your golden. It then depends on the journal turnover (how quick and often they publish per year) and how soon you get published.

In case of the r&r, the edits are going to be more major. I received an r&r which essentially told me that I needed to develop my literature section more (it had previously been a short-form paper submission, so that was fair) and that it needed more empirical support, which essentially meant running an additional experiment. If you have to do more experimental work, you're going to have to go through quite a few stages again, and that takes time. Thanks to the pandemic it took me an additional year to get the manuscript for that submission ready. Like I said, it's a process. An r&r can also be a change in analysis (running more tests, different tests or a lot of robustness checks), more theoretical review or a completely different perspective or storyline to sell the results. An r&r will require a lot of work. Also, resubmitting an r&r is not the same as resubmitting a conditional acceptance. For the r&r the editor and reviewers have to go through the largely changed manuscript again and get to review it again, as if from scratch. So it's not certain that your edits have been deemed worthy. You could receive yet another r&r or a rejection. One of my supervisors had once received four r&r's on the same manuscript. I thought it was insane.

In case of a rejection, the comments should also indicate what is wrong with the paper and how to rework it. In this case, the rework will be major. It may be so major that it's not really worth it. That decision is up to you and your collaborators. However, it is also possible that the rejection is due to the paper not being a good fit for the journal. Not in terms of ranking, but in terms of topic. You may simply want to look at a different journal and rewrite the paper accordingly, if necessary.

When it comes to journals it's also good to know that they are ranked. They have impact factors, star signs and the whole rigmarole. Your institution as well as your field of study will have a list indicating which journals are in the top (4*), just below (4), in the middle (3) and below (2–1). Aiming for a 4* journal is seen as being much more competitive and as such requires more work, better writing, amazing results and very nice reviewers. On Twitter, there are entire threads dedicated to the evil reviewer 2, as for some reason, reviewer 2 always seems to have the most comments and critiques on manuscripts. You'll see.

I've described the publication process to you. Well, actually, what I've described to you is what you need to do to submit to one journal. But if that journal rejects you, after major edits or not, you have to pick another journal. Often what happens is that people go down the journal rankings. If the 4* journals don't seem to want the manuscript, aim for journals with a rank of 4. If they also keep rejecting, move to rank 3. Some academics have the rule that if they can't publish in a rank 4, the paper is dead and they move on.

This process of resubmitting your work to different journals obviously requires major edits in case of r&r's and rewrites in case the journal requirements in terms of structure, word length or format are different. I've said it once and I'll say it again, academia is not a fast process. And neither is publishing.

In total, the time passed between the conceptualization of an idea and actually getting published has been a long time (over a year) already. And this is normal in academia. Within the field of economics, the process of publishing itself is already multiple years, so it's even longer. I'm mentioning this fact, as well as having mentioned the statistics on desk rejection to give you a more realistic idea of publishing. The idea that you get into a 3–5-year PhD and come out of it with multiple publications at the time of submitting your thesis itself is unrealistic. I'm not saying it's impossible, but it's highly unlikely. And we need to be honest about that.

If you don't believe me about this version of affaires, why not ask your supervisors? There's more chapter to come looking into some more supervisor communications. Fun!

Time Management and Multi-Tasking

I've described several aspects of the PhD process already in terms of the many things you're likely going to be doing in the several years the PhD will take you. If you are a good planner, the sheer amount of different things going on all the time may not be very impressive to you. But for someone who is not a great planner, it may be a bit confusing. Or just plain overwhelming.

I genuinely hope I haven't made you feel overwhelmed by listing the many tasks and activities and the many steps required version of a paper. That was really never my intention. My intention was to give you a realistic representation of what a PhD is likely to be like. And one of those key characteristics of doing a PhD, or doing research in academia, is that you'll likely have to juggle multiple projects at the same time. The reason for this is simple: projects at different stages might not require as much attention as they initially did, freeing up time to start other projects and further research developments. Having projects at different stages assures you of never being out of work: if your initial project is waiting for feedback from collaborators or supervisors on a draft, your second project is waiting for results or data to come in, well, then you can move onto finishing up the pre-registration or literature review for you third project. Having multiple projects at the same time also builds a buffer for one of them getting stuck, or failing completely.

The question then becomes: how do you juggle this efficiently?

It is difficult to give generalizable advice here because people's working styles tend to be very different, especially if the PhD is relatively unstructured and allows for individual working styles to flourish. But I will try.

First thing to keep in mind: there are only so many hours in a day, week and month. It is commonly known that most PhD students work more than 40 hours per week. But just because this is common, doesn't make it right. I just want to put this out there before diving into the practicalities of planning.

Initially, you will start off with a single research project. This will most likely have come from the research proposal, or out of early discussions with your supervisor. As described in several previous chapters, there are steps to going from an idea to the actual conducting of the research and to the writing up and editing of a paper draft. Some of these steps take a constant hands-on approach, such as working out the hypotheses, research questions and methodology — and designing it accordingly. During those periods, your focus will likely be entirely captured by this single project. But once you send your work for edits, checks or approval (funding, ethics, etc.), there is a gap. Depending on your (mental) state, you may want to take this gap as a break. Or, if this gap is relatively long or these gaps are becoming increasingly frequent, you may direct your attention to a second project.

If your supervisor(s) are the main reason for there being a lot of gaps in your single-project schedule, starting another project with them may not be ideal. You may want to start a project with a different supervisor (many PhD students have an additional one) or you may want to reach out to different collaborators altogether. This can be other academics at your own institution, people highly placed in your field, your PhD colleagues or even people in the industry who have companies that are doing similar research to you or have data you might want to work with. These are all valid options and can lead to amazing projects.

Let's assume you're doing a second project with a collaborator, who is an academic also placed in your field and who is more senior than you are (I've done this myself, which makes the example easier). You reach out to them or they reach out to you and you start meeting, discussing various ideas of what you could do together in a topic you're both interested in. This project will now start to have a similar progression as any other project would — moving from ideation to creation, to being conducted, analyzed and written up. What the division of labor is here is also up for discussion. Are you in charge of this project? Are they? Is this a 50/50 split? If so, who's doing what exactly? This warrants some serious communication. But if you can manage this, this will be a great introduction to what most academic research is like.

One thing to watch out for: will projects like this also enter your PhD thesis? There is a time limit on the PhD, so I do feel like there should be an increased focus on starting (and definitely finishing) projects that are valuable to the PhD thesis itself. There is nothing wrong with having side projects, especially if your plan is to remain in academia, but make sure you have enough time left for the projects that do go into your thesis. If your collaborator (regardless of who they are) is happy to have this work be part of your thesis, there'll be no issue at all. This is also very common if two (or more) PhD students work together on the same project and include it in both of their theses. What happens then is that both of them have to indicate who did what in the PhD thesis declaration at the start of the document. Do check with your department whether such a "half chapter" (meaning, you did half the work) counts as a "full" chapter for your dissertation. Some departments or universities require you to have x chapters of work that is entirely your own (with supervision of course). This type of chapter may not satisfy those criteria. Solution to this is to have it as an additional chapter or to have two of these chapters to make a "full" chapter, if collaborations are only seen as "half" chapters.

You can choose to have as many collaborations with as many different people as you like. Issue is that collaborations take time. Just make sure you keep your eye on the price: having a full and high-quality PhD thesis.

I mentioned earlier that taking on additional collaborations is a good idea if working with your supervisor(s) is going relatively slowly, but of course, this need not be the case. I have heard of supervisors who did not dedicate set times to their supervisees, but who dedicated set times to projects. So, if you have multiple projects with them, they dedicate more time to you as a supervisee, but equal time to the projects. This can work really well and ensures continuous progression on all of the projects. With meeting time reduced if one of those projects is waiting for approval of some sort.

The opposite might also hold true: supervisors dedicate set times to supervisees, regardless of the amount of projects going on. In this case, you might want to take charge of what is being discussed in that meeting and what needs to get done next to make sure those projects keep progressing.

You can also indicate that at certain stages you're going to need to have longer or more frequent meetings to keep up with the progress in all projects equally. But maybe you don't need to have this conversation at all, as you yourself are not keeping up with the projects equally either. This is not necessarily an issue: if you meet your supervisor(s) very frequently (e.g. every week), it is difficult to have made progress on five different projects in a single week. I'm sure they understand that.

Overall, I recommend having multiple projects, at different stages when doing a PhD. I think it improves workflow and ensures you don't get stuck waiting for one thing to get done with nothing else to do. It's an insurance against *dead time*, if you will. I do think it helps to have different collaborators so you can diversify your risk even further, but do continue to focus on the chapters that go into the PhD thesis. I'm not saying other work which will be for publication only is not valuable — it's incredibly valuable. However, it has much less of a deadline than the PhD thesis does. And that's the truth.

It is entirely possible that none of the previous sections is applicable to you and your PhD, whatsoever. Sometimes, a PhD isn't multiple research projects, it's a single one. This can be quite common in the humanities, where a single study of a phenomenon is conducted from so many angles it is a bookwork in and of itself, but also in the sciences, such as engineering, where the entire focus may be on creating or perfecting a certain process or product. In that case, the multi-tasking aspect of this chapter may not be as useful to you. But the time management aspect still is.

Time management is still key in a PhD. If you don't believe me go back to Chapter 20 and read it again. Because a PhD can be so structureless some people's time management just goes out the window. With a variety of possible consequences.

But maybe a more important question here is: what is time management? I think a very simple definition of time management is the allocation of time to work and get certain things done. So, how do you determine which hours, and how many hours, you end up working?

What do we base our hours on? Well, it depends. Some people prioritize other things going on in their life, prioritize those and fill the voids with the work required for the PhD. You often see this with part-time PhDs or PhD students who have a family or are still employed as well. Most (full-time) PhD students still approach the PhD as if it were a "regular" job, working 8 hours per day, sometimes even sticking to the 9–5 basics. If you know a bit about psychology, especially social psychology, you'll know that in situations of uncertainty, such as figuring out how many hours you "should" be working on a PhD, people look to others similar to themselves, who might know what to do. So often, if there is a strong leader in a PhD cohort, or simply a majority employing a certain working style (say 9–5, 5 days a week), most of the cohort will follow suit and employ the same strategy. This is part of the work culture of this cohort now. Nothing wrong with that.

Issue is, most PhD students also know people who work a lot more than 40 hours per week. Examples of people who did 60 hours or more per week easily spring to my mind. One of my friends worked at least six days a week. I still don't know when, or if, she actually took breaks. What I do know is that when she didn't work, because of Christmas holidays or whatever, and she was (supposed to be) spending time with her family, she felt guilty about not working. I too have had these feelings of guilt. Not putting in enough work, lagging behind, despite there being no objective indications of this being true.

We all have different ways of working. And we know that. We're allowed to have those differences. The PhD allows for it. Sometimes even encourages it. And yet we compare. We compare ourselves to the people around us to figure out where we stand on the social ladder. This is also known as social comparison. We can compare ourselves upward, to those who work more hours than we do, and feel terrible about ourselves. How dare we think that we're getting away with putting in "so little work"?! We can also compare ourselves downward to those who work less hours than we do and still feel terrible about ourselves. How can they get away with putting in "so little work" and we're struggling to meet our deadlines putting in many more hours?! There is so real winner in social comparison, trust me.

When I was asked to present my experience of the first year of my PhD to the new cohort of PhD students, my main message was to not compare work ethics. If I were to compare my work ethic to those of my colleagues and friends, I don't think the comparison would be very favorable for any of us. But you cannot measure your success as a PhD student in hours worked. It needs to be output based. If you get three times more done in five hours than someone else gets done in ten, good on you. If you feel like you get less done if you have to work a full ten-hour day, and this also diminishes the work you are able to do the next day, do not work ten hours per day. There is no point. You would actually reduce your own productivity. So ultimately, figure out what works for you, and stick with it. As long as you do get your work done, and meet your deadlines!

Also, you are allowed to have breaks. I strongly recommend you actively plan breaks into your work planning. Make sure to plan for research deadline, ethics applications, conducting the research, writing up the research *and taking time off.*

There is increasing pressure in the PhD to work more and more. To figure everything out early on and just keep at it. I have had years in the PhD where I worked over the Christmas period as well. For me, there was no real break. When I was not attending to my own research I was teaching or marking assignments. If you do not wish to have a burn-out at the end of your second year, I suggest you take actual weekends off, weeks off to go on holiday (or just not work) and sometimes, a nice mental health day off. Your (mental) health is what you need to get through this process. See it as an investment if you would rather not see it as a break. No need to feel guilty or embarrassed about an investment!

I would say that one key aspect of time management is that you don't end up working too much: doing work and nothing but work. I know this to be the reality of a lot of PhD students, but again, that doesn't make it okay.

This is why I'm such a fan of (artificial) deadlines, especially if they're set by people who know the PhD process and timeline. If your supervisor(s) tell you that you need to do something by the end of the month and you work to such an extent that it is done by the end of month, does it really matter whether it took 20, 30 or 40 hours a week to get it done?

I'm raising this argument not as a way to promote under- or overworking. I'm raising this argument as a way of looking at your PhD progress as a series of tasks that need to get done, rather than the number of hours that need to be worked.

I have a background in psychology so I am aware of the effects of overworking, stress, a lack of social life, and a lack of exercise on both the mind and body. If you expose yourself to this for too long a burn-out is almost inevitable. So a key part of time management is planning in breaks. Actual breaks. Which is exactly what we'll be discussing in the next chapter.

Taking Breaks

Taking breaks is an important part of efficient time management, whether you are in a PhD or not. I just keep hammering this fact home, because a PhD can be so structureless that a weekend may seem more like a suggestion rather than a mandate. I'm here to tell you that sure, sometimes you're going to have to work a weekend or an evening to get something done. It happens. However, by default, a weekend should signify time off. And you need to respect time off.

Now, a break can take many forms. And I do mean *many*. And we're going to discuss all of them!

Let's start small and work our way up. I strongly recommend you take small breaks. Small breaks here are quick breaks in between tasks to replenish your energy, get some exercise in and refocus your mind. There have been formalized ways of doing this, such as the Pomodoro technique, which is a time management system that suggests that you break your workday into 25-minute chunks separated by 5-minute breaks. After about four Pomodoros, you take a longer break of about 15 to 20 minutes. In the 5-minute breaks, you can do some stretches, get a cup of tea/coffee or have a quick chat with friends (online or otherwise) and then get back to it. For the longer breaks, you can actually watch a YouTube video or have a meal. Maybe even a quick walk?

The Pomodoro technique doesn't work for everyone. Some people find the 25-minute time chunks too short. Especially if they have to dedicate entire days to a single task (e.g. design an experiment) and don't want to interrupt their focus too often. Or maybe the opposite is true, and the work you're doing has more intuitive breaking points than 25-minute gaps. As I'm writing this book, I take a break after each chapter. And trust me, those chapters do not get written in 25 minutes. Whether you Pomodoro or you don't Pomodoro, make sure you take what I would essentially call "refreshment breaks" to get a new beverage (stay hydrated!), text back your friends/family and at least have breaks between tasks to optimize your focus.

Onto bigger breaks: do not forget to eat lunch. I'm not joking.

If you work, for some ungodly reason, 12+ hour days, this is going to encompass several of your key meals of the day. Now, I'm not going to say I approve of working those types of hours, but I acknowledge it may happen. Even if you work less than 6 hours, your schedule may coincide with "eating time" depending on how your schedule works. Now, regardless of time worked (we care about output, remember?), you need to take sufficient breaks for eating. If you work 9–5, there needs to be a lunch hour in there somewhere. If you think an hour is too much, 30 minutes will do as well. I personally always have lunch between noon and 1 pm, so I get hungry again around 5 or 6 pm, when I have dinner. Thing is, I don't always start at 9, sometimes it's closer to 10 or 11. So, I sometimes do work till 7 or 8 pm. Meaning my dinner.

It's not always breaks for eating either. If you like having the day broken up into different chunks by larger breaks, go for it. If you want to start work at 8 am, take a 1-hour coffee break with a friend from 10 to 11 am, work for two more hours and then have an hour-long lunch break with another friend from 1 till 2 pm, work three more hours till you hit 5 pm, I don't see why you can't. If that works for you, if that optimizes your focus and re-energizes you, go for it.

Also, your breaks don't need to be social breaks — I just find that social commitments make me actually take the breaks. If you're more introverted and prefer to have a break where you read a non-academic book for an hour, be my guest. I won't stop you. Just make sure that you commit as much to that break as you commit to having coffee with a friend. You get my meaning?

This type of break doesn't stop when the working day ends. This is the type of break which is also having dinner with your friends or family. Going out for a walk or cycle to get some fresh air in. That hour you do exercise, whether that's pumping weights in the gym or doing yoga. All these are breaks that are required to live a balanced and full life. So don't deny yourself those.

Scaling up again: not taking hours off, but taking parts of the day, or entire days off. I know, wild.

There will be days when all of your projects are in a state of "pause", meaning that all of them are waiting for feedback, approval, are stuck, etc. If there's nothing for you to do, or there is simply nothing of great urgency that needs happening, take the time off. Indulge. Feel like you're playing hookie. You naughty PhD student! Honestly, all jokes aside, if you do stumble upon such a magical moment, savor it and use it to the fullest of its advantages.

A scenario which is more likely to occur is the case of feeling uninspired or having a type of block. The PhD requires a lot of high-level mental work (e.g. thinking and ideation). And sometimes the brain is just having none of that. The solution to this can be doing work that requires a lot less cognitive effort such as emails, admin work, data input, planning work or any form of cleaning (equipment, data, files, actual real-life paperwork, etc.). A lot of these tasks do have to happen and often get moved to the end of the day or unfortunately, the weekend, so as to not get in the way of the "actual work". However, if you can't get to the actual work because of a mental block, why don't you do these tasks instead if you still want to feel productive. And if none of these things are urgent or you don't have the need to feel productive, well, why don't you just take the time off? Mental blocks are often a result of overexertion of cognitive resources in the days, weeks or months before. Your brain is literally asking for a break, so give it a break.

We can also assume a much less rosy scenario. You wake up and you feel terrible. You get to work, physically or mentally, doesn't matter, and it's just not going. Everything takes much longer than it normally does or it isn't going anywhere. The only thing increasing is your frustration and feelings of demotivation and self-loathing. Just stop. Close down your work, leave the office and call quits for the day. Some people can push through it, like in the previous scenario, by doing other, less difficult or less cognitively straining tasks. If you think still "achieving" something that day will make you feel better in the long run, be my guest. But with this type of day, where everything is a mess and you feel down in the dumps and simply unable, it may be an impossibility to push through it and do anything at all. So don't.

As I've said in the previous chapter, taking time off is not a waste of time that should have been spent working. It's an investment in re-energizing yourself, so you can continue working at a high level. Doing a PhD is working at a high level of cognitive effort. So make sure you invest in rest. And for goodness' sake, try to not work weekends!

If the last two of the three scenarios described above occur frequently or are occurring more and more frequently, I think it may be time to listen to your body. It's trying to tell you that it needs a much longer break.

There are countries (e.g. Switzerland, the Netherlands) in which a PhD is actually considered a job. Meaning it comes with a nice salary, set hours per week (my best friend is on a 32-hour contract) and with set times off. I mean, you have 20 days per year mandatory holidays and they do not carry over into the next year. You don't get paid for them either, so you better take them off.

In this system, the default is to take those days off, because that's what they're designed for. However, most PhD programs don't have this structure in place; there are no designated days for taking a holiday and as a result, the default function of any given day is for you to work during it. This is not a structure promoting healthy working behaviors, and you know it.

So, how do you work around this? You must have friends who have a non-academic job. Maybe your partner has a non-academic job. This means that somewhere there is a schedule that has holidays in it. If you really cannot come up with your own holiday schedule, simply steal theirs.

What may also help is to tack onto your supervisor(s) holiday schedule, granted that that schedule is healthy. I don't mean that you end up going to the same holiday resorts (can you imagine, how awkward) but that you take breaks when they do. This often means that you're on the primary (or secondary) school calendar, because most academics will have children of those ages and will be involved in caring for them, which includes taking time off during school holidays to spend with family. You can definitely use that as a guideline too. And of course, if you're feeling confident you can also totally make your own holiday schedule. I won't stand in your way!

Just remember that work is an important aspect of life, but it isn't life itself. And one thing that helps you see that is taking a break, giving yourself some space to breathe and gaining perspective on what's going on in your PhD and in your life as a whole. It really does help.

It's also a really good way to prevent burnout and other mental health issues, so let's discuss those!

Mental Health

Let's talk about everyone's favorite topic: mental health. Everyone has it, some people have had some issues with it before the PhD, and a lot of people will have mental health issues during the PhD, so let's dive into it.

To kick us off: everyone has mental health. This is not an opt-out system. Most people are aware of their mental health, as it is in its most basic form how you are feeling, and coping with those feelings. So ask yourself often during the PhD: how am I feeling? Because that question in and of itself might help you a lot. Do not repress your feelings, it never ends well.

PhD programs are renowned for their mental health issues, the most prominent ones being depression and anxiety, the latter often being fuelled by what's known as the imposter syndrome. There are reasons why mental health issues are so rampant within the PhD. It's a long-term process with little to no positive feedback, lots of critiques and negative feedback and no immediate rewards. There are ways of getting around these issues, but in essence, that's it. Add to this that during a PhD you are working long hours, for low pay, in an environment which almost exclusively focuses on difficult-to-obtain outputs, constantly facing uncertainty in terms of career prospects, and you've got yourself a situation which is a breeding ground for mental health problems.

I will outline several mental health issues in this chapter, their likely causes, and how you can begin to deal with them. One big disclaimer here: I am not a trained psychologist, clinician or therapist, I'm just trying to help you out in a non-binding, non-professional way.

You probably noticed in Section 2 that I prepared you for receiving rejections when applying to PhD programs. The rejection rate for PhD programs is relatively high, because of the limited number of places and the high demand for them. However, the rate of rejection in everything that comes during and after the PhD is even higher. Let me explain.

When in a PhD, you will be competing for even more scarce resources, such as funding bids (grants), journal article spots, conference presentation slots, and you'll be competing against every type of academic, even those who have much more experience than you have. As a result, especially in the beginning, your chances of "winning" are relatively low. This means a lot of rejections from applying to those things.

Now obviously, your supervisor(s) are supposed to be there to help you with this process. They give advice on how to do funding and conference applications, and they'll edit your writing to the extent that your paper is competitive enough for the journals you're submitting to. However, most supervisor(s), or actually most people, will tell you exactly what's wrong with your work and what you need to change to get it into a better state. What you're getting is a lot of negative feedback. Because when you're asking people how you can improve, you're telling them to tell you where to cut the dead wood. You're not really asking them to outline everything that's already good with the work you've done. So what you're getting is mainly negativity. I'm not saying it's not useful. I find most feedback useful. I'm just saying that from a mental health perspective, hearing nothing but negative things: "this isn't right", "you need to change this", "this isn't relevant" or "redo this section" does have an impact. And it's not a positive impact.

And all of this feedback and help doesn't negate the scarcity of the resources you're vying for.

Positive feedback is one form of reward, in this case, a more immediate reward. Humans are built in a way that we seek out rewards. It's how we learn new things and continue to be motivated to do new things, build habits and learn.

That's a second issue within the PhD: all the rewards are uncertain (with a high chance of rejection, or disappointment if you will) and they are placed on a much longer timeline. There are no immediate rewards because there are no (or very few) short-term projects. Whereas you could satisfy a sense of achievement by obtaining good grades in undergraduate and master's degrees, this doesn't work in a PhD. You can achieve smaller tasks, or take steps that are required for your research to be successful, but what happens is that there are so many steps in a project and that there are so many projects, that you're getting lost in the mountain of work that still remains to be done.

The PhD as a process essentially starves the mind of immediate rewards, which is something the mind needs. It craves it. I'm not making this up, this is actually very basic psychology and neuroscience. Now there are two ways to cope with this: (1) either you find more intrinsic rewards and learn to enjoy "the fruits of your labor" (but mainly your labor) differently, or (2) you're going to have to find your immediate rewards somewhere else.

Option 1, finding intrinsic rewards, is hard. You're going to really have to approach your work differently. As I outlined earlier, people struggle to actually celebrate reaching certain steps in their research, or completing certain tasks, because there is still so much work to be done. The intrinsic way of approaching this is to celebrate every form of progress. It takes a much more Machiavellian approach to work, where it's not the level of progress that matters, but the fact that there was progress at all. The fact that most people can't do this is a contributing factor to the high levels of depression in academia.

Option 2, finding rewards somewhere else, might be a more viable option for you. And this is also why I keep telling you that you need a life outside of your PhD. This is why I wanted you to get to know the social life on campus from the very start. Sign up for social clubs and sports clubs, be friends with your colleagues, go out, have hobbies, etc. It means you can derive pleasure and rewards from those. Having goals besides the PhD work, whether that's seeing your friends once a week, running 5k, finally baking a nice tasting banana bread (my specialty), finishing a good book or being able to do a difficult move in yoga are also achievements. The brain craves achievements, so find them wherever you can!

If you as a person are not feeling like you're achieving anything, you're opening yourself up to a load of mental health concerns, of which one is the imposter syndrome.

The imposter syndrome: the idea that somehow, somewhere, someone made a mistake, letting you into this PhD program and you're just fooling everyone into believing that you're remotely capable of being a PhD student, but in fact you are an imposter. At least, that's what's going on in your head.

The imposter syndrome is a rather nasty thought pattern that is difficult to annihilate as it's grounded in something people have been doing since the dawn of time (or rather the dawn of humanity, remember social comparison?!). Remember that? To repeat: social comparison is the psychological approach of valuing yourself relative to others, to determine where you fall in the hierarchy. Wolves also do this to determine their rank in the pack, it's instinctive. We are able to do this in two separate forms, upward and downward. In downward social comparison, you compare yourself, as a whole or on specific traits, to people who you judge as being "below you". This can easily make you feel good about yourself and support the notion that you're doing well or are ahead of the curve or better than average. Upward social comparison is the opposite, where you compare yourself to those who you judge to be better than you. This can be done to motivate yourself and determine how far you still have to go, but this also often just makes you feel crap, and like an imposter who doesn't belong in the position they're currently in.

Given that social comparison is almost instinctive, it's very difficult, if not impossible, to switch off. But what does help is putting things into context. Comparing your achievements to all the achievements of someone who is 10 years your senior (in age or experience) will not help you feel better about yourself. Obviously.

It's also always helpful to discuss these things, especially as a lot of people suffer from this, and it's the illogical truth that we are kinder to others than we are to ourselves. Having a couple of colleagues or even friends in similar positions (those can be the same people) to discuss this with, to vent to and to seek out solutions with is really helpful. It'll surprise you too that people who you might look up to are mentally in the same place as you are, and might hold you to the ideal you hold them. They might think you're doing amazing and that they're doing badly, whereas you believe the opposite. The truth of the matter is, we can never fully know what's going on in someone else's mind, just as they cannot know ours. Talking is the only way to get it out and progress out of the imposter syndrome into the belief that both you and your work deserve to be in the position you currently are.

Another aspect of the PhD that I've already mentioned is the lack of structure. Some people really cannot handle a lack of structure well and overwork as a result of it. This sends some people into overdrive, as a way of placating their constant worry of not meeting imaginary deadlines and expectations of what should have been done already. This is a recipe for burnout. Especially if this type of anxiety is accompanied with cutting out all non-work-related activities, such as sports, a social life and relaxation. In Chapters 20 and 25, I've outlined how to impose structure on your life, which can easily be done in agreement with your supervisors. That will take some of the pressure off because no one can work 24/7 without the repercussions presenting themselves several months later. In Chapter 26, I've outlined the importance of taking breaks. I meant it.

Overworking is not the only possible consequence of lacking structure, underworking is also entirely possible. Although underworking is often not associated with anxiety and burnout, but with depression. A PhD is an isolated experience: you're mostly on your own, doing your own project and conducting your own research. So, it's unsurprising that it's easy for PhD students to feel as if they are constantly alone; that there's no one with them; no one who cares about what they do, how they do it and how they are doing as people. To some really anxious people, this may be a relief and may motivate them to take a week off once in a while, but to others, this is so highly demotivating that they try to get away with the bare minimum, and need constant monitoring or interference from others to keep going. If this is the case, you need to indicate this to your supervisors and take it from there. They should have dealt with this problem before, and support you accordingly. Refer back to Chapters 20 and 25 if you need any help with this.

I'm not saying that anxiety or depression, at any level of severity, can be cured by having heart-to-heart conversations with your supervisor(s) and them (trying to) accommodate you. However, making people aware of your situation and having them support you in a way which allows you to at least keep going workwise (assuming that this is the right thing to do), can be very helpful.

In the next chapter, we will discuss several different forms of failure. Failure or perceived failure (not the same thing) will impact your mental health. It may make you feel worthless, useless and like you don't belong in the PhD program (imposter syndrome again). This is not true. Your worth is not derived from your PhD alone, which is exactly why you need to have a life next to your PhD. Do not make your PhD your entire life, because if something does go wrong, which it inevitably will, you won't be able to bounce back as easily. Sometimes, things don't work. Bad things happen. Don't beat yourself up over it. Go see your friends, have a vent, have a whine and a wine or go for a run to simply get the frustration out. Whatever you do, deal with it. Do not repress these feelings. Communicate your feelings, talk about them and discuss them. Maybe in the same talk mention how this feeds into your overall feelings about the PhD, the work and yourself in relation to those. Talk, vent, allow yourself to experience negative emotions and then determine what is making you feel those negative emotions. Sometimes they simply come from a single incident. That's valid.

Sometimes those emotions are coming from an accumulation of several incidents. If that's the case, are those incidents tied together? Are they re-occurring? Is there a pattern there that can be observed and hopefully broken? If so, how would you go about that? Is there someone who can help you with that? I'm a rather practical person, if I see something that keeps making me feel awful, I'll try to remove it from my life, or at least limit my exposure to it.

Cutting something out isn't always an option. However, the desire to do so is a clear signal that something isn't right. What is making you miserable? How is it making you miserable? Can it be dealt with? Often this is again a conversation to be had with friends, colleagues and supervisors. The latter again should have seen this before; they do tend to have experience with a wide variety of PhD students.

As I've mentioned hundreds of times by this stage, if it's your supervisor(s) making you miserable, clearly define how and why they're doing that. Sometimes this can be communicated to them, there might be room for discussion and compromise. Sometimes you and your supervisor are a mismatch and you're suffering from that — discuss it and see where it takes you. And sometimes supervisors are just vile people and you need to switch.

To take some of the heat off the supervisors, because I really am giving them a bad rep., there are other possibilities for suffering from mental health issues. But the key here is to identify what they are. If they're not your supervisor(s) nor the structure (or lack thereof) in the PhD, what is it? Do you feel alone? People really do underestimate how lonely a PhD can be and often is. Your work is your own. Your hours are your own. Your progress is your own. Your mental health is your own. You are the only person really monitoring what's going on, on a day-to-day basis, and it can be maddening and saddening to feel that way. I hope in writing this book

I can prepare you better for it, so it doesn't come as much of a shock when you get to this stage. In general, I'm writing this book to try to give you a better understanding of what a PhD is before you start one. A lot of mental health issues also arise from the gap between expectation and reality.

On the topic of expectations, are you doing what you'd expected you'd be doing? A lot of PhDs start off with the idea of curing the world of something (cancer, poverty, gender discrimination, etc.) and receiving a Noble Prize for it. After their first (couple of) years and just having to jump through a lot of hoops and get started laying the groundwork for their research, most people have already *slightly* adjusted their expectations. After more years and more hoops and actual results coming and things not working as they should have, most people adjust their expectations quite a lot more. By that stage, the mere idea of getting anything published will already seem like a massive achievement (which it is) rather than aiming for that Nobel Prize. This process happens to everyone, but it can really dent your self-confidence. Again, this is okay. It happens to most if not all PhD students. Talk about it, and make sure to have a life outside of the PhD.

This chapter is getting longer and longer but I do want to make sure I mention most mental health issues that I've experienced or known others to have experienced throughout the PhD process. In line with the previous topic, there is the shock to the mental health system when you realize how academia really works and the true prospects you're looking at.

Now, this sounds a bit dramatic, but for a lot of people, the inner workings of academia are quite hidden. And academia hides them on purpose. Most PhD students will not stay in academia. That's not in any prospectus, trust me, I've checked. But you couldn't sell someone a PhD with that statistic. Now, why is this?

Over the years, universities have been hiring more and more PhD students. The cohorts are getting bigger. There are several reasons for this, but I don't want to make this chapter any longer than it needs to be. You just need to know that the cohorts are getting bigger and bigger. However, the increase we see in PhD students being hired has not extended to the rest of the university: most universities do not as a result hire more post-PhD students into positions such as post-docs, research/teaching fellows, assistant professors, etc. The growth in the number of those positions per university has not kept up and has remained relatively stagnant. People don't mention the pyramid shape of academia…

What does this mean for you as a PhD student? Well, it means that you are competing against an ever-increasing pool of PhD students for a small number of positions. This is incredibly competitive. Now, academia has always been competitive, so this isn't much of a surprise. But no one is honest about how competitive it is, and how you actually beat the competition. With the limited positions available, people at the top universities who want to get hired as a post-doc (or other after PhD equivalent) will aim to go to top universities. If they don't get hired at the limited positions available there, they'll apply to the next tier of university, so a tier lower, say the second tier. As a result of this, they're crowding out second-tier PhD students and pushing them down to lower tiers as well. This is how the PhD competition works. And yes, a lot of it is determined by the ranking of your university, although publications and networks matter massively as well. Issue is, these variables are correlated with each other.

Once you realize how difficult it is to get an academic job, either before or after applying to hundreds of different institutions, you may have a full-blown meltdown. It is really difficult to manage endless job applications with your PhD being a full-time job as well. And constant rejections (as is often the case) can be really disheartening. Luckily, or rather unluckily, you're not the only person going through this, so there are people who understand your experience, and can maybe help you with it. This is really a difficult process to go through, and I'll elaborate more on this in Chapter 33.

Now, there are more severe cases of mental health issues that can occur during a PhD, and some of these issues can turn more severe as well, especially if you continuously try to repress them and don't address them as they occur. If you feel like, for whatever reason, you're really not coping, are having intrusive thoughts of worthlessness or can barely motivate yourself to do any work for prolonged periods of time, seek professional help. As I've said before, I'm not a mental health expert nor have I experienced every mental health issue in the book nor have I gone through every possible experience to be had in the PhD, but if it's bad, it's bad, and you need to help yourself.

Reach out to the university's mental health services, they must have them. Maybe they are specific to your department even. If you prefer to not engage with the university for your mental health requirements, find an organization working providing mental health services in your local area. They really have caught on to the idea of a lot of students and academics needing this type of support, so trust, there will be one. Try to seek professional help in whichever form you can. Whether it's one-on-one, group or online therapy. Therapy really has helped a lot of people. And I'm fully aware of the fact that there is a large number of PhD students within my own university using the university's counseling services.

Another point I'd also like to mention is the timeline for this. Your mental health doesn't just collapse. At least, it often is a more gradual process of deterioration. As I've told you in Section 1, it's a good idea to constantly check with yourself how you're feeling about the PhD, your work and yourself, adjusting your initial expectations as you go. If you continue this introspective process, you will start to notice more subtle changes much earlier on and will start to notice the deterioration of your mental health. You may be able to ask for help much earlier as a result of this. If you can nip the cause(s) of your worsened mental health in the bud, through talking, through telling people how you feel and through communicating to others what they can do for you, then that is incredibly helpful. I'm not saying that this will fix all your problems, I'm just saying that they reduce the load of a lot of them, and maybe even help you realize the need for professional help much earlier on, saving yourself from getting to a much darker place. Because as much as I love and recommend therapy, it's not a quick fix. Therapy is a long process of recognizing what is and isn't working for you, in every aspect of your life, why it isn't working and how to cope. That can take years. So, if you're realizing you're struggling, and you think you might need some help, reach out and get the help that you need. Start that process for your own sake.

Last, I'd like to reiterate a final point: you're a student, you're learning, and you're trying your best. You're also human, and some experiences are really hard and can take a toll on your mental health, to the extent that we're better off asking for help. If that's you, ask for help. The PhD might be a lonely experience, but there's no reason to be completely alone for all of it.

Failure

Failure is an integral part of the PhD. Actually, failure is an integral part of life. It's a bittersweet learning experience of misery and growth. And quite frankly, it's inevitable. It's also a massive factor impacting mental health, which we discussed in the previous chapter, so it's definitely something to keep an eye on.

No one likes to fail. Ironically, there are many ways of failing in both life and the PhD. Failure in the PhD can range from losing a day to writing useless code that your supervisor could do in seconds, to losing several months or even years working on a project that just isn't working, or didn't produce the expected results and has just been rendered useless, for one reason or other. Whatever the case, you will experience failure to some degree. There will be things in the PhD that aren't working. And this chapter is on how to deal with that.

There is no job in the world, nor any aspect of life, in which people do not fail. Let's get that out of the way. This is in no way, shape or form unique to the PhD. It's just that within the PhD, due to it being a rather lonely experience, you can feel completely alone in your failure, not knowing what to do or who to turn to, and that can become a problem.

Let's assume for a second we're having a *failure light* situation (like low-fat milk). So you spent a day doing something that didn't work out. It's frustrating, definitely. But in the grand scheme of things, what is 24 hours really? Same for a week of working on something, say coding up an experiment using JavaScript, that just isn't working right for some reason. It may not work in the way you thought it would, it may be lagging or just bugged beyond belief. The key thing here is, it's *only* been a day, a few days or a week.

The important thing is (1) that you admit to yourself that things aren't working to the extent that they should, (2) that this does not reflect poorly on you and that this should not be taken personally, and (3) that you need to seek out help. Those three steps will get you out of an absolutely fruitless mindset and where you need to go next. Also, they'll make sure that several fruitless days won't turn into several fruitless weeks or months. Because losing several months in a PhD is a slightly more serious problem. That is no longer *failure light*, this is taking on *full-fat failure* proportions.

Asking for help is not the easiest thing to do. The first step in asking for help is identifying the problem itself: why isn't something working? It'll definitely help having defined this issue, both for yourself and for the person you're asking to help you. On the topic of the person you're asking for help: who do you turn to? Often, in a PhD, you'd assume that your supervisor(s) are your main point of contact, but that isn't always true. Especially if you only speak to your supervisor(s) once every month, this might not be the best solution. So who do you turn to?

There is a hierarchy within the academic system, whether academia wants to admit to it or not. In this hierarchy, there are several people just like you: your colleagues. It's a rather low-risk approach to simply ask one of your colleagues whether they have ever encountered the issue you've encountered or have experience doing the task you're currently attempting to do. No shame in asking, it might lead somewhere. Maybe there is a colleague of yours who can help you out: win! Now do keep one thing in mind: you can easily ask colleagues to help with a *failure light*. Something you have been stuck on for several days will probably take someone who actually knows what they're doing only several hours max., and that is a negligible amount of time to help someone else with their PhD, without it being too much of a loss to their own. Showing up with months of mistakes and things not working (*full-fat failure*) might be too much of an ask, unless a colleague of yours really has a lot of experience with the task at hand and can sort it out in several days max. In that case, you better be prepared to give them back those several days in the form of helping them out.

On a sidenote, if you're doing a project in which it's clear that you don't possess all the skills required, either sign up for courses teaching you those skills or teach yourself via online tutorials, etc., or turn the project into a collaborative effort with one of your colleagues who does have these skills. This repays them for their efforts more directly by having their name on the paper. Just an idea!

Going back to the hierarchy, if there's no one on your own level, you'll have to move up. Directly up from a PhD is the post-doc level, so you can reach out to them. Post-docs come in a variety of shapes, so just look out for anyone with the title "fellow" and you should be good. There might also be other people in the research group who have experience with the specific problem you're stuck on, such as assistant professors, or the lab managers and technical support staff. Especially the latter has seen most problems at least once, so they really can help! Best way to approach them is either directly face to face when working together, going past their office (to set up a meeting, not immediately barge in with your problem) or popping them an email politely asking them for help.

If there's absolutely no one in your immediate surroundings who can help, turn to the internet. I'm assuming that you would've googled the problem before even asking someone else and checked every possible forum for help, but how about just throwing your query online? You can use Stack Overflow, Reddit, Quora or a field-specific forum for your queries. Academic Twitter is also always a good shout. I'd recommend hanging out in the Academic and PhD Twitter pages anyway, they're really a wealth of information and support.

You might be wondering why I seem to be so averse to recommending you to simply ask your supervisor(s). Whilst I would recommend this in general as a first step, because that's what they're there for, I can imagine that some students really don't want to. I do understand that completely. And sometimes, you can't wait until meeting your supervisor(s) to sort out the problem, so these are the ways around that!

To exemplify all this advice with my own experience: my main struggle has always been coding, whether it's for analysis or experimental purposes. I've had a colleague who is an econometrics wizz help me out with the analysis, way before my supervisor did. I've also had to build an online experiment using JavaScript, which our Behavioural Science Lab Manager helped me out with a lot, as well as a kind stranger from Twitter who had run something similar and had actually created a small online tutorial on it. There are always people wanting to help, you just need to ask nicely. In the end, my supervisors made some small comments and edits on the progress, but all in all, they were impressed with me having gotten it done. The fact that I got it done was the main thing that mattered to them. Whether I'd had help wasn't particularly relevant.

I would like to put a massive disclaimer about asking for help out there: it's never bad, weak or stupid to ask for help. An important thing to keep in mind is that you're a PhD *student*. Being a student, of any level or capacity, means you're studying; you're learning. So if you need help, that's just part of your learning process. No shame in that!

Now, I've predominantly talked about *failure light* types of problems, or at least what to do if you feel like you're *getting* stuck on something. This is an important sentence so please read it again, and check the *italics* for the correct emphasis. This sentence is important because if you deal with *failure light* problems as they arise, they often do not spiral into *full-fat failure*. And it's the spiraling we're trying to prevent here!

Spiraling, or moving from *light* into *full-fat* problems, means we're moving out of the domain of having "lost" days or weeks (we haven't lost them, they were a learning experience) and moving into the domain of *having been* stuck on a problem for months or even years. Given that a PhD is "only" several years, this is not a timeframe you want to mess with.

Sometimes it's difficult to recognize *failure light* as actually being problematic. The most obvious and most frequent problem encountered by PhD students is with their supervisor(s): they never seem to have time for you, or cancel meetings at the last minute, or you never seem to agree on anything, or they don't listen to your suggestions and keep bulldozing you with their own ideas. They might be good ideas and you can progress on them, and progress is still being made despite them not meeting you. So is there really an issue?

I'd argue that all of these things combined are several dark orange flags making one huge red flag (because that's totally how the color wheel works). If one of these happens as a one-off, maybe make a mental note of it and move on, but if several of these happen continuously, what you have is a supervisor (or multiple) who has no interest in you or your project, and will not help you learn, grow, progress, publish or graduate. More on supervisor communications of this kind in the next chapter.

Now, it's not always the supervisor who's the problem (I promise). Sometimes a project you've been working on for a long period of time just doesn't produce the results that you were expecting. And then I mean the type of results you really can't do anything with — they're so out there, unclear or they just don't mean anything — and make the project impossible to publish. This sucks, but often also couldn't have been prevented. If you feel like it could've been prevented ask yourself: how? Again, it may have been a supervisory issue: they ought to have known better. But if they could've known better because of existing research on how something should or shouldn't be done, you should've been aware of that research too. So don't be too eager to point a finger, it might not get you anywhere besides aggravating your supervisor.

What really matters in this scenario is that you figure out what to do with these results. Is there any way to salvage them (without p-hacking)? Can you run a different analysis on them that makes more sense? Would it be better to run the study again and do the whole (or parts of) the project again, but maybe with slight tweaks? These are questions to ask and discussions to be had with your supervisors, but maybe also with other people who have experience with the task, topic or project you're doing.

Now *full-fat failure* isn't always your fault, meaning it's not something you could've salvaged. I've recently heard of a bio-med PhD student whose suppliers reached out to tell her that some of the enzymes they had supplied her with might have been faulty. It wasn't even a certainty whether they had or hadn't been faulty. They *might* have been. If they are faulty, it means several months, I think about half a year, of work has been rendered useless as it literally cannot be used. These things do happen, but when doing the viva (PhD thesis defense) you will have to explain what happened, and this will be taken into account. But it'll hamper career progression as this work can most definitely not be published.

There is, unfortunately, also *full-fat failure* which may have been partially, or fully, your own fault. Part of the PhD project of my best friend is to develop a game which allows patients with certain forms of brain damage to retrain their brain. I won't go into specifics of the topic, it's quite hardcore. Now, this PhD is a structured project with multiple PhD students attached, where my friend is the neuroscientist who tests the effect of the game on brain functioning. However, there are other positions, of which one position was tied to the actual development of the game. So, one PhD student was responsible for actually coding up the game itself.

I feel like you may be able to guess where this is going. That specific student got stuck on a problem within the code and couldn't figure it out.

Instead of telling people this, and receiving support, either from the people directly affiliated with this project or others who were affiliated with the department, they stayed quiet. During the weekly meetings when asked about the progress, the PhD student always indicated there having been progress and being sure to meet the initially set deadline.

Obviously, as the initial problem never got resolved (or even mentioned, really), the rest of the progress didn't happen either (from what I've understood game building is a rather bottom-up process). With every meeting, this poor PhD student got more and more behind, constantly increasing the gap between reality and expectation. After a number of these meetings, the supervisors, in addition to the team as a whole, wanted to see actual progress. They wanted to see the game, which by this stage, should have been in a workable format. It wasn't. The PhD student had to come clean: there was no game, just a lot of code that didn't work. In the end, the PhD student was fired and the team had to look out for someone else to build the game. They did not take on another PhD student, they took on someone with a background in game design to build the game as a short-term job.

The total delay for the project, which was a structured project with a clear deadline and finite funding scheme, was 4 months. Which means that the other PhD students on the project, including my best friend, are suffering a 4-month delay to their PhD project, which likely will be unpaid, because of something that isn't their fault. That's what I call *full-fat failure*.

Now, I'm not saying this is completely the fault of the PhD student. Should they have mentioned this issue earlier? Definitely. Should they have sought out help? Definitely. More help? Probably. But where are the supervisors in all this? Why was this discovered so late? I know some supervisors are laid-back, but quite frankly, this behavior raises some serious eyebrows with me.

All in all, do yourself a favor: if you're stuck, let someone know. Preferably someone who can help you. I know I mentioned in previous chapters that if one project is "on pause", you can work on another project and progress that one to optimize your time management, but I didn't mean that you could just let one project die a slow death. Especially not if that project is key for your PhD thesis or even your PhD team!

In the scenario described above, as in most cases, *full-fat failure* starts out as *failure light*. There's just a single thing that isn't working; that is throwing you off and can't be fixed in a day. Reach out, ask the Internet and ask your friends. Tell your supervisor(s) that you've stumbled across a problem, that you're giving yourself *x* amount of time to find a solution for it and if you haven't managed to find a said solution by that time, that you're going to need to meet to get it sorted out. That is literally their job. Don't hide small problems and then ignore them. They escalate. They always do.

When it comes to *full-fat failure*, it's going to leave a mark. You're more than entitled to take a few days or weeks off to just recuperate from your loss because it is a loss in some sense. It's an excuse as good as any to take a break. The most important part to remember is that just because something failed, doesn't mean you failed. You're not a failure, it could've happened to anyone, it doesn't reflect poorly on you. When you've dealt with the emotional aspect, it's important that you start analyzing your next steps as soon as you feel able to. You have what you have. Whether that's results that don't make sense or code that isn't working (yet!). It's definitely not perfect, but it's yours, so what do you do with it now? Start asking questions and having discussions with the right people. Some things can be salvaged. If it turns out it's really not salvageable, discuss whether it should be mentioned in your PhD thesis at all. If your supervisor thinks it's better off left out, without the risk of you not having enough work to display, cut your losses and move on. It's rough, but it's necessary. A PhD may seem like a long time, but that time is gone in a blink. Trust me.

I've hinted at the mental health impact different forms of failure can have throughout this chapter. There will be an impact. The PhD in general will impact your mental health, it just does, due to its very nature. In the previous chapter, I've outlined how to deal with several aspects of mental health, and if you are struggling as a result of (perceived) failure, what you can do to help yourself.

Things become a lot more serious if you constantly feel like a failure. If your sense of imposter syndrome is continuous and symptoms of anxiety and depression are increasing or already rampant, you need to seek out help, immediately. One such person you're going to have to reach out to is your supervisor, as you need to communicate your state of well-being to them and the way this may be, or has been, impacting your work. We'll discuss that now.

Talking Supervisors (Again)

I wouldn't be surprised if you got tired of this advice, but you need to talk to your supervisors. Have you spoken to them yet today?

All jokes aside, open communication is very important. I don't mean that you need to tell them of every fart, but you do need to talk to them on a regular basis. And the reason for this is the shift in dynamics that you often see in a PhD as it progresses.

In the very beginning, especially if you have little to no work experience, the relationship between supervisor and supervisee is almost employee–manager like. Not in a sense that they control your every move, but in the way that they know much more about doing a PhD than you do. They also know more about the departmental requirements (courses to do, deadlines to meet, mandatory training, etc.), as well as know more about the research topic or methodology. As a result, you still have much to learn from them. When meeting and talking about what needs to happen next, they point you in a direction, and you follow that direction. Even if their direction is a guideline rather than a mandate, it's probably a good idea to at least check it out.

This is the type of relationship which I've also described in Section 3. They very much hold the upper hand as you're starting to develop and grow into the PhD. It's quite normal — as long as it doesn't take any toxic forms (Chapter 17).

This type of relationship, however, will not last very long, and it's not supposed to either. As you progress in your PhD, you do more research on your topic, your methodology and how to set up your own research. Again, some PhD programs are more structured than others, so this type of "preparation" and the freedom to choose your own niche can look very different for each PhD student, but the gist of it is this: you'll soon stop being a rookie.

Now you might continue feeling like a rookie, but you're not. Once you've read up on the empirical work done in your field, or specific topic, you're at least a topic expert, in the theoretical sense. This means that you can discuss the ideas that your supervisor brings to the table and bring your own ideas to the table and have them discussed. You're no longer writing down their words and taking them as gospel. It's also your game now.

This transition, as I've said, is meant to happen. Your supervisor(s) should aim for you to become an independent researcher, as that is the goal of the PhD. In the end, most of the work and the ideas (the latter depending on the rigidity of the PhD structure) should be yours, with the support of your supervisors. In the end, the discussions should very much be you coming up with ideas, implementations, methodologies, etc. and them raising counterpoints and arguments, having a discussion, reaching an agreement, you being happy with that agreement and taking it forward and them signing off on it. That's what a PhD should look like, again, depending on how structured it is. Some PhDs don't allow for this, but you'll know that much further in advance. Also, just because your PhD is more structured doesn't mean you won't grow as a researcher nor does it mean that you won't be able to have more meaningful discussions with your supervisors about the how, what and why of the research. That's still very much part of the package.

As I said, supervisors are supposed to help you grow into an independent researcher, however, they are also, to some extent, supposed to support you in your more personal growth. Now, I'd like to emphasize that a supervisor is in no way, shape or form a mental health professional, so I don't mean this in a therapeutic sense. I mean this in a "if things aren't going well, and this is impacting, or a direct result of, the PhD, you should be able to tell your supervisor(s) about it" kind of way.

In the previous two chapters, we discussed mental health and failure. These two aspects are central to the PhD and are largely inevitable. You will have moments of struggle, both with your work and with yourself. If these struggles impact your work or are a direct cause of your work, it is important that you communicate this to your supervisor(s). Their reaction to this type of message will tell you everything you need to know about the quality of supervisor you've got.

Supervisors, or people rather, can react in a variety of ways to "bad news". Their PhD student struggling with part of the work is a form of bad news, the project being stuck somewhere is bad news. All of this is bad news that you're bringing to them. In the case of being stuck with work, if they're not offering you any form of help or at least guidance as to where to find help to continue making progress, you've got yourself a supervisor who doesn't seem to care much about the project. That's not good. The idea of a PhD supervisor is that they are at least interested in the research you're doing together. That's really the bare minimum. If you find that they're just never actually invested, the best solution may be to take on an additional supervisor or additional collaborators. I've already discussed this option in the previous chapters on supervisors, but it is entirely possible that your initial supervisor doesn't have enough time, or in this case, interest, to support your work as a PhD researcher. It's probably a good idea to find someone who does. And if you're wary of switching supervisors, well, just add on another one, or add on more collaborators!

The previous paragraph exclusively describes a bad reaction from your supervisor to bad news relating to the work itself, but obviously, their PhD student suffering mental health issues is also bad news. This topic, mental health, is still tricky to a lot of people, PhD supervisors included. If their initial reaction is to shoot the messenger, blame you or simply do not listen to you, you've got yourself a supervisor who doesn't care about you as a person. It's still entirely possible that they care about the work and will provide help with that, but this may be the only thing they care about. They have no real interest in supporting you as a person. It's more difficult to know what to do in this scenario. Tacking on additional supervisors who would almost exclusively look after your mental health and provide pastoral care is hard, and maybe also rather inefficient. Personally, I would recommend seeking out professional help in this case. It's up to you to decide whether this is a supervisor you want to continue working with. The idea that they "at least care about the work" may be sufficient enough for you to keep going with your research, but with complementary support from elsewhere. That's not a choice I can make for you.

Maybe it's not mental health or issues and feelings of failure that are making you re-evaluate your PhD work and your relationship with your supervisor(s). Maybe it's something else entirely. Maybe it's you being exploited as cheap labor. Which is something that, unfortunately, happens in academia quite a lot.

When you start the PhD, you're a junior who still has to learn a lot. That's what you're there for, to be developed into an independent researcher, able to design and conduct your own research. Issue is, some supervisor(s) seem to have missed the memo on that specific goal of the PhD. Some supervisor(s) seem to be more keen on keeping you down, so they can continue keeping you as an RA (research assistant), contributing to their research, where your name may or may not appear on the paper, and your contribution may or may not be recognized. This is a role very different from a PhD researcher. An RA is there to assist, as the name indicates. A PhD student is there to become an independent researcher. You can see where the friction would arise.

If you're starting to feel like you're being used rather than developed, you might want to communicate this to your supervisor. Again, this is an expectation thing. If you expect them to turn you into an independent researcher, yet they have no desire or intent of doing so, there's a serious issue there. Luckily, there are solutions to this:

1. you can switch supervisors;
2. you can continue with your current supervisor but also add on additional supervisors;
3. you can continue with your current supervisor but start different collaborations.

You have seen all of these solutions before, but I would like to reiterate how to go about this, as these options are different at the start of the PhD than they are in the middle or towards the end of the PhD.

The first solution is more drastic than the second and the third. So, let's work backwards, starting with the third to build up to the first.

In Chapter 17, I've already discussed the option of taking on additional collaborators if you feel like your supervisor is not getting you where you need to go. Taking on additional collaborators moves all of your focus away from one project with one person (the initial supervisor) and divides it across several projects with several people. This will require some better time management, but it'll also build a buffer: if something goes wrong with a project, you'll still have the other projects to move on with. It can give great peace of mind. This option is the investment equivalent of not investing in a single stock but buying entire portfolios to spread risk, known as risk diversification. However, what you're doing is taking on more and potentially different types of projects. So you're taking on more work. Having collaborators who are not your supervisor(s) at any stage of the PhD will not raise eyebrows. Academic work is often collaborative. Issue is, if it's not work progression but support you need, this option might not be as valuable to you, because collaborators are often project specific.

Option two does more in terms of support. Taking on an additional supervisor adds someone to the team who not exclusively focuses on the work, but also on you as a researcher. In the example in Chapter 17, this was someone who would meet with you more frequently to develop your work and ideas better, and quicker. It can also be someone who takes out more time for your psychological needs. The PhD is a mentally draining process and having support is great, if not required. An additional supervisor may take on this type of role as well, assuring you of yourself and your work, in addition to discussing your research. However, I do feel obliged to mention that finding an additional supervisor in the middle of a PhD is more difficult than finding one at the start of the program. When reaching out to potential additional supervisors you're going to have to be honest about your program progression and your motivation for wanting an additional supervisor. And they have every right to say no. Obviously. Not a lot of people are interested in providing predominantly pastoral care. Rather than supervising, this is often more associated with mentorship or mental health support. More about that in Chapter 31.

Continuing on the topic of taking on an additional supervisor, you should probably ask yourself what you want them to do. If you're running into issues with your initial supervisor while being much further ahead in the PhD, the kind of issues I'm foreseeing are not *light* issues. I'm expecting issues as outlined above, where the supervisee is slowly being turned into an RA rather than an independent researcher or has their deteriorating mental health completely ignored. The question then becomes: what can an additional supervisor do for you? And sometimes the answer may not be what you want it to be. Sometimes, the initial supervisor and you are too different and this comes to light just a little too late in the PhD timeline. This is, lightly put, incredibly unfortunate.

It is also entirely possible that your initial supervisor turns out to be toxic. That their manipulations go far beyond keeping you down as an independent researcher. In that case, what can an additional supervisor still do? Provide relief? Show you that there are better people out there?

If you're at the very end of your PhD and your initial supervisor's mask has accidentally slid off, I can imagine you might have a preference for sucking it up, getting the degree and moving on with your life. I really can. But if there are years to come and this person is the personification of an academic nightmare, is adding another supervisor enough? Can they be enough for you to minimize contact with your initial supervisor, without too much retribution, to finish your PhD? I'm asking this because it might be for the benefit of both your mental health and your work to still seriously consider switching supervisors. Issue is, that is also a nightmare of a process.

As I've outlined in Chapter 17, there are behaviors which are so inappropriate they are a one-way trip to HR. Regardless of whether you feel like your problem fits the "standard HR package" or not, talking to HR if you want to switch supervisors relatively late in the PhD is a good idea. Why? Because they know much more about it than you do. Also, if your supervisor is seriously vile, you may want to have a paper trail for their behavior.

Now, I'm going to be very honest, I've heard horror stories where PhD students got "dumped" by their supervisors who decided to retire without much of a heads up or who decided to switch institutions and not take their PhD students with them. In most of these cases, the PhD students did end up with new supervisors and they ended up being fine. But I've also heard the stories of PhD students who tried two switch supervisors and ended up being fired from the PhD program by the university, as the supervisors tried to blame the student for what had gone wrong to deflect blame away from themselves. The PhD student was suddenly without a job, and getting a new PhD after being fired from one is almost impossible. There were no repercussions for the supervisors.

Academia, like any other job sector, has bad apples in it. However, that doesn't mean you have to stick with a bad apple. You can get out and you can switch. But, and it's a big but, this is not an easy process whatsoever. And if things escalate, you will have to get HR involved. Another thing that you can count on is a delay in your progress. It's very unlikely that you'll be able to finish your PhD research in the original time allocation.

Quick note of caution: All of the things I've discussed in terms of switching supervisors are mainly for those PhD students who are in PhD programs where their topic and funding are not tied to the supervisor. For those in a structured PhD there may be more complications. Switching supervisors in a structured PhD, where the structure is tied to the topic which is often tied to a grant, which is tied to your supervisor, switching means quitting.

To move away from the rather dramatic and depressing topic of bad supervisors, switching supervisors and its repercussions, most of the time what you'll be discussing with your supervisors are next steps in terms of your research as a way of facilitating the next steps in terms of your career. Which leads me to the next chapter: what do you want from the PhD, exactly?

What Do You Want from the PhD?

We've discussed a lot of things that could possibly go wrong in the PhD, but I think now it's time to turn to making sure the PhD is going right for you.

Now, what is and isn't right for you doesn't necessarily depend on the PhD itself. It depends on what you want from the PhD. And that's what we're going to discuss now.

Staying in academia

The PhD, in its very essence, is a program designed to create independent researchers. Originally, the idea was that those researchers would finish their PhD and become academic faculty. That was the idea, at least.

Without providing too much detail, the academic job market is no longer able to sustain and maintain the influx of PhD students. It has become a lot more competitive. Many more PhD students are being trained than there are follow-up positions, such as post-docs, fellowships, assistant professorships, etc. If you're dead-set on staying in academia, you may want to design your PhD in a way that allows for you to be incredibly competitive in the academic job market. So how do you do that?

Different aspects of the PhD are valued differently. The main "currency" an academic has are their publications. This may sound harsh but it's the unfiltered truth. If you come out of the PhD with a publication in *Nature*, or *Science*, the chances of being hired into a post-doc, fellowship and even an assistant professorship are a lot higher. I would even recommend you start out applying to assistant professorships and move "down the ladder" initially, with a publication of this rank.

Now getting an article into a top (4*) journal is difficult, and setting up that type of research is time intensive. It is easier, and often quicker, with PhDs that are structured or semi-structured, where the topic and (part of) the methodology have been pre-decided and you're being guided by very hands-on supervisor(s), or have a multitude of collaborators who are all very involved, and preferably (more) experienced. We see this a lot in the natural sciences: papers have multiple collaborators and have a relatively quick turnaround time, as compared to economics, where there is the "job market paper" which is a single-author paper (by you, obviously) and the turnaround time is much slower, and the peer-review time is also immensely slow. Economists are also known for their high rates of rejections and revisions, as well as their not-so-nice feedback. So do look out for the formalities in your field, because they do matter and will determine a large chunk of your strategy.

Knowing the formalities and limitations of your field, plan accordingly. If you can get a great publication with your supervisor, in the time required, go ahead with that. If you're starting to realize that going with your supervisor isn't the right route for you, find different collaborators. Look at people in your field, your department or simply your colleagues. Find out which route works for you, and go for it. You can also do all these routes. As outlined in Chapter 25, you will likely be managing multiple projects anyway.

On the topic of balancing multiple projects: you won't come out of the PhD having published everything you've worked on during the PhD. You might not come out of the PhD having published anything — that is also quite common. What you have in this case are working papers.

A working paper is a manuscript which hasn't been published yet but is close to that end goal. Now, this is not that useful a definition, because "close" can mean a variety of things here. Let's go with what you need to know for your CV: on your CV, you will have a section with published papers; you may want to have a section with submitted papers, including r&rs (really not required) and a section with working papers. The latter are all the projects you are working on that haven't been submitted yet. Obviously, there does need to be some type of manuscript ready, these aren't supposed to be projects in the conceptual or very "rough draft" stage. Having this on your CV does signal the type and amount of research you have been doing during the PhD. These projects are also what you'll continue to work on if you stay in academia. Often, post-docs (or other fellowships) are used to publish more work from the PhD to become more competitive for (assistant) professorships.

Another part of staying in academia, on top of the publications, goes back to "hot" calling. You will still have to apply for your next position, even if you are the most well-published PhD student in the history of PhD students.

As I've said many a time already, I'm not a fan of "cold" calling — sending in applications to people, groups, departments and universities at which you know no one and they don't know (about) you either. I think the chance of failure is just really high there. What does help is if you did know specific research groups or even specific people, so that they can notify you when positions are opening up in their group, or even hire you directly. So how do you go about that?

There's a variety of ways to get to know someone or even a whole research group. Getting to know an academic often relies on attending the same conferences, reaching out and meeting up during these conferences, talking about shared research interests and seeing if collaborations are possible. Don't worry — all of this can also be done online and via email if needs must. That is probably the simplest way of getting to know an individual academic.

Now, getting to know a research group can be an extension of the process described above. In addition to getting to know the individual person, you also go "visit" them. Research visits are an actual thing, and can take up to several weeks. If you want even more time with the group, you could do an exchange. These are also quite common and can easily be justified if the research done with this group, or the individual, is key to the PhD research. Check with your department or own group what the process is for this in terms of duration, eligible institutions and funding, but it is definitely a good way of getting your foot in the door with another group.

The reason why this works is because they know you. That really is the key aspect of "hot" calling. If they know you, they know who they're dealing with and have been able to find out whether you, your research and your work ethic are compatible with the group and the group's goals.

You've essentially made yourself a low-risk hire. And (most) people are essentially risk-averse!

Now, unfortunately, even if you have networked and do know a lot of people at a lot of places, and have done the visits and exchanges it is still possible that things don't work out. I'll admit, if you have actually applied this strategy I'd be surprised if something didn't work out, but it is possible. In that case, the applications do become a numbers game. I'll talk more about this in Chapter 37.

Moving into industry

So the academic job market is a tough nut to crack. This may be a reason for you to orient yourself towards industry partially or completely. You may have other reasons to want to go into industry after the PhD rather than the uncertainty of the academic job market: perhaps you have issues with the academic system as a whole, the timelines don't suit or you just want a completely different working style. Whatever it is, you can transition from a PhD program into industry, it just warrants some "editing".

As I said before, a PhD program is designed to turn you into an independent researcher. Although originally targeting academia exclusively, these days are long gone. PhD students are flooding into industry. And although we may hit like a tsunami, that doesn't mean that industry has any idea as to what to do with the water.

Industry is very different from academia. If there's no one in the companies you are targeting that has a remote idea of what a PhD is, you might want to help them a bit. PhDs are often seen as extended forms of education by those who know little about them. As a result, they aren't counted as work experience. If you're determined to go into industry, you're going to have to change their perception of your "degree" and get them to look at it as "research" or even more generally: "work".

So how do you do that? Well, it helps if you conduct industry-facing work. What are the trends in your field's industry counterpart? What are the hot topics? What are the developments they are looking at, worried about, or preparing for? What are the issues they are running into? Target that as a topic. This might be looking at diversity and inclusion in recruitment practices (management and psychology), applications of a new tool or machine or actually building the thing to improve inefficiencies in a process (engineering and physics), or understanding refugee migration and integration (humanities and international relations). This shows that your work can be applied practically or has strong ties to current ideas and provides you with the expertise in a topic industry is actively focusing on. Keep in mind, I'm using the term industry to mean "not academia". The latter topic (refugees) would also be studied in government — so industry does not mean corporate here by default.

In line with this clarification of definition, it also helps to know in advance which type of companies, or even which exact companies you may want to work for, and target them accordingly. You can reach out to these companies and ask to collaborate on research: they may have specific problems they'd like to address, or they might have data you might want to work with. This can go either way: you almost become a consultant in the first case, or in the second case, you'll be given a dataset to scavenge to your heart's content (with possible limitations). Either way, make sure that you've got clear agreement on your ability to conduct the research in a rigorous and academic way, with the inclusion of using the work for both your PhD dissertation as well as a peer-reviewed publication. Especially the latter will warrant some serious discussion, as you're going to need to use this material, regardless of the results found, which may go directly against the company's interests (possibly).

In addition to using your company collaboration(s) directly for your PhD research, I also know of PhD students who became consultants during their PhD programs. After having gained (some) expertise in a topic useful to industry, they reached out to companies promoting their expertise and skillset, and actively started consulting. This work is *in addition* to the PhD and not as a function of it. This obviously does warrant some serious time management skills.

A slightly more radical approach to obtaining work experience is the option of internships. There is the possibility of pausing the PhD and taking up an internship in industry. This is essentially the equivalent of doing a research visit or exchange, however, in this case, you'll have to pause the PhD, as you'll no longer be conducting your PhD research, which you would very likely still do during an academic exchange. I know plenty of PhD students who have done internships to get either work experience or a better idea of what "working in industry" actually entails. You can look for internships specifically targeting PhD researchers (they exist, just google it) and make sure to check this with your department or university as well, as programs like this often have direct links with universities to recruit PhD students — it's just much more efficient this way. You can also apply to general internships, which do not specifically target PhD students, and get your experience in this way. This option is very likely more reliant on your doing the legwork in terms of finding the opportunities, but your university may still be able to help you out here. If you don't ask you'll never know!

In the scenarios above, I have described how you as an individual can go about attracting industry attention to your PhD and get work experience during the PhD. But who says you'd have to go at it alone?

If you knew from the get-go that you wanted to move into industry after your PhD, you could play a long con and select your supervisor on the basis of this very fact: which academic has strong ties with industry? If you find someone like this, they'll very likely be able to launch you into company collaborations, have data available or do consultancy themselves, and give you a leg up there. Don't worry if you didn't know from the very start that you needed an academic like this, you can take them on later as an additional supervisor, collaborator, or even as a mentor — more on the latter in the next chapter!

Obviously, if you are targeting companies who hire PhD students actively, everything described above should be much less of an issue: they don't need an explanation of the PhD being work, they know. But that doesn't mean the rest of the advice isn't still valuable.

Also, the type of firms that often know much more about PhD programs are firms heavily rooted in doing research themselves. This may require another shift in focus. Most non-research industries will very likely not care about publications or exact topics much. Research-based firms will place a higher value on this, so keep that in mind too!

Similarly to networking in academia, you'll have to network in industry too. Reaching out directly to companies to set up collaborations or data sharing is one way, but that strategy doesn't scale too well: you can hardly do this with more than five companies, you'd have no time left. I also don't really count this as networking. Networking in this case is making sure you know a wide range of people in industry (again, this can also mean government or non-profit, this is not just corporate). And to do that, you need to go where industry goes!

So, where does industry go? Well, that really depends on your field, or even niche, but industry also has conferences, meetings, workshops, seminars, etc. Research what, when and where these events are and make sure to attend. If possible, although you're probably not exactly an "industry leader", try to present at these events. If your research directly links to the topic at hand, this will be a good way of getting your work and your name out there.

Transitioning from academia (out of the PhD) into industry is becoming more and more common. If you want more resources on how to do this, make sure to check #altac on Twitter. This stands for alternative academia or alternatives to academia. It's filled with resources on how to become successful in industry, regardless of what that industry may be.

Doing both?

It is entirely possible that at the start of the PhD or maybe even for most of the PhD itself, you've got no idea where you want to go. Or, also possible, you started out thinking you really wanted to go into academia, but have realized after experiencing academia that it really isn't for you or vice versa: you've actually quite enjoyed academia and have decided to stay but decided so relatively late into the program. Or, you want to be an academic, but the job market is just working against you, and you now have to consider industry. Whichever way the wind blows, you need a plan.

Although I named this subsection "Doing both?", I don't think applying all of the strategies outlined above is really feasible; it's unlikely that you're able to set up company collaborations with many other academic collaborators who are very hands-on and can turn around publishable work relatively quickly. If you can and this is an option thanks to your supervisor(s) or network, do it. I genuinely think that's great and hits two birds with one stone. But most PhDs won't be so lucky.

Again, the idea of a PhD program is to turn you into an independent researcher. Try your best at doing academic research, try to set up (academic) collaborations, go for research visits and attend a lot of conferences. I recommend you do all of this early on as a way of getting to know academia from a variety of perspectives: different people (collaborators), different places (visits) and different topics and approaches (conferences). By doing this early on, you'll find out whether academia is the place for you in terms of your own wants and goals. If you're still not sure, I do strongly recommend doing an industry-based internship and seeing if that's a better fit. If it's not, ask yourself why it wasn't: did you not like the company or aspects of the company or was academia simply more your style? Regardless of the answer, you'll know how to progress from there.

Now, it's entirely possible that your predicament doesn't come from your own wants and desires but comes from the context you're in: a bad job market. By this stage, if you really want(ed) to become an academic and have essentially followed the strategy outlined above, yet that didn't work out, it's going to become a numbers game. You'll have to do many more applications, which will include a lot of cold calls. You may also want to talk to your supervisor(s), if you haven't already, explain the situation to them and see where to take it from there. But, very likely, despite wanting to become an academic, you will have to start looking into industry as well, granted that you'll have to pay the bills and may not want a gap of several months on your CV.

I know the scenario I just described is very far from ideal. Applications like this take up a lot of time, which is why I dedicated Chapter 25 to it as well. The only real advice I can give is: try to be certain about what you want out of the PhD early on and tailor the PhD to that goal — a lot stands or falls with good design.

One thing that may help you a lot in shaping up your PhD is a mentor: someone who has (slightly) more experience than you do and has gotten where you want to go. They should be able to tell you how they got where they are now and how you can do it too!

Mentoring

When entering a PhD or, realistically, entering any type of job or career trajectory, it is difficult to establish at once what you should be doing, what you want to be doing, and how to do it. Often, there is no roadmap. And even if there is a roadmap, is that the right roadmap for you? Does it lead where you want it to go?

In the PhD program specifically, your initial guidance is provided by the rigid standards of the first years, which are often taught. You know what to do, when to do it and how to do it. The taught part of the PhD is similar to the latter part of a bachelor's degree and any form of master's degree. You have courses, seminars, lectures and deadlines. You've seen these hoops before, you know how to jump through and you know that jumping through them will get you to the next stage: the actual research part of the PhD. The reason we joined in the first place.

As soon as this part kicks in, our reliance shifts from the structure created around us to doing our own thing. For some people this is ideal. Others need more guidance. Either is fine. For those who want more guidance, it is natural to turn to their supervisor(s). Your supervisor(s), having done this rigmarole before, should be able to provide you with the basic guidance: what to do, how to do it and by when it should be done. This should be enough to get you started and meet the invisible standards of the PhD program.

To check whether you're on the right track, there are plenty of people around you who are, or have been, in the same position. So, there's lots of feedback out there if you're looking for it. Even if you're not looking for it, you'll likely still be exposed to it. In the common areas, you'll hear conversations float by of other people's success, failures, frustrations and trajectories in general. This shapes your opinion of yourself and your work too!

Now, when it comes to building an idea of yourself and your work, it helps to have an idea of where you want to go. That's what we discussed in the previous chapter. If you want to do what your supervisor(s) are doing (be in academia, work towards tenure, be in tenure, etc.), your supervisor(s) can become your mentor(s). Especially if you vibe well together and they are good, caring and supportive people, this is a very nice coming together of roads.

If it turns out you and your supervisor(s) don't actually work that well together or they are so busy they can't really add supporting you more to their curriculum, you can take on a collaborator for further research, but that only solves the research aspect of the issue. We have discussed running into this issue back in Chapter 17.

So what can you do? Well, you might also want to look at taking on a mentor.

A mentor is someone who guides and supports you also on a more personal, or more career-oriented level, rather than just with research or the PhD. Mentors tend to be people who you can look up to, who are ahead of you and often in positions that you'd like to be in.

Mentors need not be people who are twice your age and have already reached your end goal. Sometimes, that is not that helpful. The reasons for this are varied. First, as soon as you are not a cis-gendered, rich, heterosexual, white, Western male there are far fewer people to pick from if you're aiming for someone in tenure about twice your age. Because the majority actually has those characteristics. This makes their experience a lot less useful to you, because you have an added layer of your experience as a woman, non-white or non-any-of-the-characteristics-just-mentioned. Their experience can never be yours, as sad as that is. Just keeping it real here.

In addition to the characteristic divide, someone who got tenure several decades, or even just one decade ago, is facing a very different kind of academia than you are. Academia, despite it having turtle tendencies, has actually rapidly been changing, with hiring more and more people at the bottom levels and opening up fewer and fewer positions at the top. It's essentially become a pyramid-shaped pressure cooker. Someone who has recently, say in the past 5 years, gone through this market and got where you want to go next, probably has a lot more current insights into what's what than someone who obtained that position 30 years ago. Just saying.

Mentorship becomes even more important as soon as you're deviating from "the script". Rather obviously, your PhD supervisor(s) are in academia and as such have (predominantly) followed the academic trajectory. Likely, they know very little about any other trajectory at all. So as soon as you decide you don't want to be in academia, but want to develop into a highly trained researcher in industry, who do you turn to?

Before I place all of academia in an ivory tower, there are quite a few academics in my circle (keep in mind my PhD was at a business school) who do have strong ties with industry. They either run a consultancy business on the side or most of their research is industry focused or industry driven (e.g. their data is from industry). Some academics might have had a long career in industry before they decided to transfer to academia. Some still do both. It's those types of people that you'll be looking for!

Another way of going about this is to find someone who has a PhD and transferred into industry. Reach out to them and ask them about their experience. How did they do it? Was it difficult? What should you look out for doing a similar move? Do they have people in their network who can help you further? These are not strange questions at all. Chances are, the person you're talking to has asked similar questions to the people they reached out to. Or maybe just wished they had.

Keep in mind, you reaching out to anyone is just you asking for help. Most people are perfectly happy providing you with their experience and some advice. You don't really go up to someone you don't know and ask them to become your mentor. Mentorship is something that often develops after multiple interactions where the person that is ahead of you continues to help you; giving you pointers and moving you in the direction you want to go. This need not be an official agreement, this can be rather casual. These meetings can be super infrequent, where you just reach out when you want help with something, or they reach out to you to check in on how you're doing. Do keep in mind, their time is likely limited, so don't make this a one-way street. Do emphasize that you're grateful for their time and that if you can help them, add to their life in anyway (e.g. teaching for them, doing research together, actual collaborations) you'd be very happy to do it. It'll likely be much appreciated and the offer is quite likely to be taken up.

As I've described it above, mentoring can be really quite casual and informal. However, there is a more formal version of mentorship, and that is being enrolled in a mentoring program.

If this is something you're interested in joining, or at least curious about, literally type into Google the name of your university and "mentoring" or "mentor program" and you should be able to find all there is available in milliseconds.

There are advantages to being enrolled in such a program. Given that it has a formal structure, the mentor is very likely an experienced person who has helped many a PhD students' progress into the next stages of their career. However, this may at the same time be a disadvantage, as this is someone who has experience mentoring, but may not have the experience that you were looking for specifically (e.g. having transitioned into industry). This type of mentor is selected for you and is not a person of your choosing. If you want something very specific from a certain type of person, I'm not sure this type of mentorship will give you that. But there's no harm in trying!

There are also quite a few mentorship programs out there for women and other minorities, which will target those specific experiences as part of the mentor program. Hearing the experiences of others who have gone before you, that you can actually (partially) relate to, may be very helpful in your journey. However, if that's not what you're looking for, then these programs may not be for you.

This chapter is in no way, shape or form an exhaustive list of where to find a mentor nor what types of mentors there are, but I just wanted to emphasize that just because you have one, or even multiple, PhD supervisor(s), that that is enough. Sometimes you need more. And a mentor can help you in many more ways, which might be more meaningful towards your career progression in the end.

Another thing to keep in mind, although mentors are often focused on both professional and personal growth, whereas some supervisor(s) may exclusively be focused on professional growth, mentors are not a replacement for therapists or counselors! If you are struggling with mental health issues, a mentor is often not the answer. When seeking out professional help, do seek out the right professional.

Knowing When to Quit

The original question of the entire first section asks: "Should you do a PhD?" There is also a slightly different version of this question that we are going to address in this section: "Should you continue doing your PhD?"

In the previous chapters, I've outlined a myriad of things that can occur in a PhD, particularly, what can go wrong. Sometimes, when these things go wrong, they don't just make a mark, they hit like a meteorite and leave a crater. In this chapter, I'm going to address indicators that the PhD isn't working for you, as is, and what you can do about it.

You're crying at the best of times

"It was the best of times, it was the worst of times". This sentence can put people to sleep in an instant (sorry Dickie). But it alludes to my purpose. It is easy to continue something, even if it's hard, if it's going well.

Let me take myself as an example. I don't enjoy doing statistical analysis in R and I try my best to avoid it (to absolutely no avail). But once I'm at it, and it is actually going well, the tests run, the models work, the graphs seem to actually represent what they need to, etc. I don't notice that I have just done a full day of coding. I end my day feeling pretty good about myself. I'm kicking this PhD's ass. Booyah!

Now imagine the opposite. Nothing freaking works. I run into issue after issue. Variables can't be found, data have been read in wrong. Models run slowly or not at all, and I have forgotten the basic grammar of structuring a graph. I've been at it only 3 hours, and I am willing to commit genocide on everyone who ever thought R was a good idea. I feel worthless as a PhD student, and I'm doubting whether I'm even made of "the right stuff". The imposter syndrome is becoming stronger and stronger.

Now, these examples are incredibly common (the latter occurring way more often than the former). What you have to watch out for is when you are having doubts even at the best of times. If things are going well, and you're still crippled with doubt, or continuously experience negative feelings towards the PhD, such as anxiety, depression and exhaustion (see Chapter 27). These are pretty good indicators that something isn't working. And maybe you should think of a way out. This is exactly why I quoted that tweet at the start of Chapter 1. There's no shame in finding a way out if it's not working. Just be able to admit that to yourself.

This is of course an issue you can only run into once you're actually in the PhD. But that doesn't mean there isn't a way out. The first year of a PhD course can often be transferred to an MSc, MPhil or MRes degree. Now the issue is that the first year is still rather structured (courses, frequent meetings, administrative obligations) and represents a lot of novelty and change: you might notice your incompatibility with the PhD only later, say in the second year or even after that. But the initial offer still stands: you can transfer it into a master's degree, granted that your PhD has a taught aspect.

Don't fall into the sunken cost fallacy. Just because you have already put in 2 years or more that were largely miserable doesn't mean the next years have to be miserable too. It's absolutely alright to admit that a PhD just isn't for you. Take the master's degree, figure out what you want and move forward. Quit to move on.

Managing mental health

Another aspect which leads to a large drop-out rate during the PhD is mental health, and it really does not get mentioned enough. I did address this already in Chapter 27, but honestly, do not underestimate the toll the PhD can take on your mental health. If you are in a very fragile mental state that currently, or when getting worse, warrants serious and immediate treatment, sort that out before doing a PhD. Because the chances of you being able to juggle this and getting out of bed to work are slim to none.

Another mental aspect that you need to take into consideration is the lack of structure within a PhD program. If you have a need for structure, yet feel unable to create that for yourself (think of people on the Autism spectrum or the OCD spectrum), the PhD is going to hit you where it hurts. If you don't have coping mechanisms for this in place, I would strongly recommend a lot of preparation before starting a PhD, because it will be very aversive to your mental health. You might want to read Chapter 20 again to figure out more about structure, and maybe also Chapter 25 on time management!

Now, these arguments for really considering when you want to do a PhD can seem as if I'm profiling based solely on mental health, and I'm not. At least I'm not trying to. I'm trying to paint an accurate picture of what the PhD is going to be like, and some pitfalls that you should really prepare for. By no means am I trying to say: "Depressed folks and autists not welcome". If there were no autists doing PhDs, the entire field of physics would have collapsed decades ago. The same goes for people with depression and PhDs in psychology. It's a joke, but statistically not too far off!

I have plenty of colleagues and friends in PhD programs that are neuro-atypical. They're doing just as well (or just as badly) as everyone else is doing, but they had their baggage under control when starting. This means they were either being treated, had been treated, or were aware of what works and what doesn't work for them. If you are nowhere near these stages in your mental health journey, I wouldn't recommend starting a PhD. I'm not saying anyone who has ever experienced an episode of worsened mental health should never do a PhD. It's just that PhD programs seem to trigger something that worsens overall mental health, for the majority of people. I can hardly stop you from doing a PhD, but please do take this into account. It would be such a shame if you had to pause or even stop your PhD, because you simply weren't prepared for this. But obviously, a rapidly deteriorating state of mental health and mental wellbeing is one hell of a reason to quit the PhD. Or at least pause it for a bit. Which is what we will be discussing next.

Quitting, pausing or switching?

If parts of the PhD really aren't working for you, it may seem like removing yourself from the situation as quickly as possible may be the best way forward. Quitting seems like a good option. But before you make the decision to quit, there are several other things you can consider, which I strongly recommend.

You can pause a PhD. Freeze the funding, freeze your current enrollment and do something else. This something else can range from doing an internship, holding a job (work experience) or working on personal development. The first is quite commonly used if the PhD student knows that they want to move into industry after the PhD, to solidify ties. Additionally, it can also be used to get a better taste of industry or a specific job sector in general. Through pausing your PhD and gaining this experience, you might actually figure out that the PhD is not for you and quit it entirely, using your newly established ties and job position to continue in industry. The exact same goes for holding an entirely different job for a longer period of time. Both options can be used for gaining experience and informing the decision to continue the PhD afterwards or still quitting. It's also a safer option than cold-turkey quitting the PhD and then looking for jobs, as you will still have a back-up option if the job search is not going well.

Another reason to pause the PhD, unsurprisingly, is mental health concerns or other unexpected circumstances that affect mental health, such as the loss of a family member. In the former case, if your mental health would benefit from taking a break from the PhD for several months and you can manage to do this without massive financial impact, this can be a really good option. There's no shame in giving yourself a break if you're in the privileged position that you can do so. There's also no need to feel guilty about being in that position of privilege. Use whatever you have to your advantage. In the case of the latter, universities and the respective department a PhD is with have lots of experience with their staff dealing with emergencies, or even loss. There will be a standard protocol in place that will also apply, even if slightly modified, to PhD students. So you can pause your PhD and take the time you need to deal with the other aspects of your life.

It's also entirely possible that the PhD is impacting your mental health from within; the issue is the PhD or part of the PhD itself. In that case, pausing might not fix that issue, and switching (parts of) the PhD is recommended. Switching, however, is done for a very different reason than pausing. The reasons for pausing a PhD are temporary in nature, whereas the reasons for switching parts of the PhD or the PhD as a whole, hint at recurring or permanent issues.

An example of switching is to switch topics or methodologies. This can mean shifting from one topic to another, as you have already seen in several of the previous chapters. Both my friend and I shifted, or switched, topics, moving from voting behavior to medicine adherence and from saving behavior to the effect of payment methods on personal finance management. It has to be mentioned that these topics remained in the same field (behavioral science) and were conducted with the same supervisors. This switch, especially if the specialization of your supervisor is rather wide (has fingers in a lot of pies), need not be an issue whatsoever. If the PhD is relatively unstructured, this happens quite a bit. This is not an option for more structured PhD programs, where the PhD student either adheres to the exact program or won't be allowed to continue.

With methodologies, you have to watch out a bit more. If your initial supervisor works with one method exclusively, yet you want to move onto another one, you might have to find yourself a new or an additional supervisor. You can have multiple, so this is again more of a shift, rather than a switch. The same can go for a change in topic, where a small change might mean an additional supervisor rather than a full-on switch. A more extreme topic change might lead to you having to switch supervisors entirely though.

If you want to, or rather, have to, switch supervisors, this is not as difficult as you think. What you need to do is be clear with your current supervisor and indicate the issues. If they see your point and you come to a friendly agreement, they can recommend you to different academics who can take over. This is the best-case scenario, as their approval and following recommendations indicate that this was just a mismatch on a topic or method level, rather than a much more personal or insidious issue. Also, if you're really not keen on "stirring the pot" and want to remain with your initial supervisor, you can just take on additional collaborators on projects with different methodologies or topics. A friend of mine who recently successfully defended her thesis is a great behavioral data scientist. Her thesis consists of three papers which focus on the computational modeling of three entirely different phenomena. My thesis on the other hand focuses on a single topic but explored from different angles with several different methodologies. She had several collaborators next to her supervisors, I didn't (at least not for the work in my thesis). PhDs come in all shapes and sizes.

To take it even further, sometimes you might even want to switch universities. Again, not necessarily as difficult as you think. Some universities have collaborative partnerships set up between them. I was in one such collaborative network, which was called the Network for Integrated

Behavioural Science (NIBS). This is a collaboration between the University of East Anglia, Nottingham and Warwick. You would be able to switch from one of these universities to the other if you think the respective research group would be a better fit for you and your topic. This may be because of a single person working in that group, that would simply make a better supervisor for you. Because most people in these collaborative networks know each other quite well, this is again not that controversial a move. One warning here, you'll have to go through a set of re-application processes to make this happen.

You're probably wondering: why do I get such a long list of alternatives? Well, the reason I'm mentioning these alternatives is that quitting a PhD will have consequences. Terminating a PhD in the first year often (but not always) will give you a master's accreditation. Within academia, this signals that you have stopped a PhD. In industry, this signal is not as clear and just looks like another master's degree. Moving into business from here is easier. But in academia, it's quite likely that within the next round of applications and interviews, if you decide to re-apply to a (different) PhD, questions will be asked about what happened there, and you're going to have to prepare a nice-sounding story around that. And I do mean a NICE story because universities are not keen on taking on students who have quit a PhD before. It's a dark orange flag for them.

If the PhD program does not default your unfinished PhD to a master's degree, things become a bit more difficult. To put it nicely, this won't look that great on the CV. You now have a gap there if you leave the PhD out, or, as mentioned before, you have an unfinished PhD there.

A friend of mine has had to quit her PhD (neuroscience) because her supervisory team was absolutely impossible to work with. They never showed up to meetings, forgot ethics and funding deadlines, weren't aware of application requirements and were all-round awful. The supervisory team also happened to be married, where one partner used to be the PhD supervisor to the other partner (this is a massive red flag on multiple levels). My friend complained to the head of the department, HR and several mediators before deciding to quit her PhD, as it became apparent that the group, the department and the university in general were unwilling to support her and tried to protect the supervisory team to the best of their abilities, despite this particular supervisory team having already had a previous PhD student quit on them. It was clear whose fault it was and that they were ineffective supervisors (and that's putting it nicely).

Does this story have a happy ending for my friend? So far, not really. As she quit her PhD, she was in a state of severe emotional distress and needed several months to recuperate, while also looking for new PhD positions. But as I've mentioned before, universities don't like people who have quit their PhD programs and often she didn't even make it through the first round. The specific topic she wants to work in requires a PhD, so this wasn't something she could really opt out to begin with. To keep afloat financially, she started looking for jobs based in industry, which was also extremely problematic. The PhD program she was in did not convert back to a master's degree, so she had a gap on her CV which scared off employers as well. All in all, this was a real nightmare, and I don't recommend it to anyone.

Talking about supervisors (again!!!), they do tend to make or break a PhD and there are different scenarios in which continuing to work with a specific supervisor is absolutely impossible and just not advisable (Chapters 17 and 29). The scenario that springs to mind is obviously that of (sexual) assault.

If this happens to you, first of all, I'm so sorry you had to go through that experience. Second of all, as distressed and desperate as you are now, think very carefully about what you do next. As disgusting and disappointing as it is, and although you are the victim, your research group, department and even your university will likely treat you as a liability. There are many great organizations working to rectify this gross injustice, but as things stand, this is the most likely scenario of what's going to happen.

From the experiences of several of my friends, try switching before you quit. Or pause the PhD to figure out what you want to do next, and whether that still involves academia at all. If you want to continue doing a PhD, pausing and then switching (supervisors, most likely) is still an option. And a better option than outright quitting.

As difficult as it may sound, and I can promise you that it is difficult, I would strongly recommend securing a different supervisor, research group, or a different PhD altogether, before making any other moves, such as prosecution and litigation. How you decide to handle the case after you have secured yourself a new route to move on past this awful experience is up to you.

I would like to put a very strong disclaimer here. I am not a mental health professional, nor am I in any way shape or form capable or trained in dealing with victims of (sexual) assault. I'm simply telling you about the experiences of several close friends around me, and how this impacted their PhDs and further careers.

Doing a PhD Is Not Enough

One job of your supervisor(s) and potentially also your mentor(s) is to make sure you have a realistic expectation of both the PhD and the job market you're entering into. This is to say, they should have told you that "merely" doing a PhD is not enough.

Disclaimer before we even start, as I know the title is nice and controversial: I'm not here to tell you that your work isn't valid, that your research isn't good enough or that you should be side hustling next to a full-time job, which is what a PhD is (when done full-time of course). I'm not trying to make you feel bad or inadequate. That's not the message here.

The message is that when it comes to finding a job after the PhD is over or, more likely, when looking for one during the PhD, "just" having done the PhD might not get you the results you had hoped for. It might not get you any results…

So what am I saying here? Well, you're going to have to do things next to the PhD. Now to most already over-worked PhD students, this sounds like a nightmare. And I get it. But it's really not that bad. Let's dive into why the PhD itself isn't good enough, and what you can do about it.

When it comes to getting a job, which is what I think you are aiming for straight out of the PhD (preferably after a well-deserved break, if you can manage it) you need to know people who can get you these jobs. I have written about "hot" vs. "cold" applications before, and I don't recommend the latter. Apply somewhere where they know either you or your research.

You can spot the immediate issue here: how do you get people to know you or your research?!

If you want to continue to be an academic, the aim of the game is conferences. Go to a lot of them. All of them. This allows you to present your own research, meet people who are in similar fields (so you can more easily direct your job search) and the most important of all, network! Whoever said academia was a lot less networking than corporate lied! So yes, conferences are where it's at (Chapter 22)!

Other opportunities to get to know more academics are to research who is in your field (Google Scholar will show you published results) and to reach out to these people/research groups. Maybe you can collaborate? You could set up research during the PhD that could flow into a post-doc. Who knows? The world is your oyster.

No need to "just" collaborate at a distance. As I've mentioned before, PhD programs have exchanges and research visits too. You can reach out to such a group and see if they have an interest in taking you on for a couple of days (visit), weeks or even months (exchange) to work together, let you get a feel for them as a group, the department, the university and their research as well. At the same time, they'll get a feel for your work and you as a person as well. If there's a connection, and if you're a good fit, when there are positions opening up, you'll definitely be at the top of their list. And that's exactly where you want to be!

This way of "sliding" into a research group is especially useful if this is one of the groups you'd want to continue working for after your PhD is finished. You need to make sure people know you and your research before the PhD ends. It's time to get your foot in the door, and you can't do that early enough. Maybe a foot isn't even enough, throw your whole body through the doorframe and see what happens.

If you want to make the switch into industry, you're going to have to go beyond conferences, research collaborations and other academic meet-ups. Because you're currently in academia and not industry, you are 1-0 behind. If you've got no previous working experience, you're about 5-0 behind. If you do have previous working experience, you can go through this route. Dive back into the old network and let your colleagues, peers and friends point you in the right direction.

Unfortunately, if you did the PhD to help you switch fields, this might not be that useful. What you can do is attend events and webinars that companies are organizing that are semi-targeting your field and research topic. As such you can meet them face to face (or via Zoom, etc.) and establish a connection. You can pop them an e-mail after such an event as well, to connect more deeply. And to make sure they still remember you in a week's time. There might be some freelance work as well but to pull that off you really need to sell yourself!

Some PhDs I know are worried about not having enough work experience to make it into the industry. And as I mentioned before, having work experience does help a lot. So what can you do? Well, what they have done is launch out a call to be a consultant in their field on the side. They take on the jobs they want to or at least take on the type of jobs which they feel they can manage timewise. That way, they slowly gain more work experience, gain some more useful contacts, and are slowly moving into industry!

So far in this chapter, there should be nothing new. Chapter 30 discussed most of these options already and did so in much more detail. However, I find this to be really important, so I thought I'd reiterate it. Additionally, there are other ways of growing your network, but they might simply be a bit more "out there".

From personal experience, I have grown my network slightly by going to conferences and joining different research networks [such as the Network for Integrated Behavioural Sciences (NIBS)]. I'm sure your field must have some inter-institutional partnerships. These are really useful, join them! But if I'm being really honest, the lion's share of my network comes from my writing. And I don't mean my academic writing. I mean the writing I do on my blog (Money on the Mind). Writing my own articles about behavioral science, personal finance and life as a PhD student and promoting them on all my social media have gained me a rather large following, which I otherwise never would have had. My following grew even further when I also started podcasting (Questioning Behaviour Podcast). I haven't published any academic research yet. So what would people have found about me? Almost nothing. And this is an issue.

If you're invisible online, or practically invisible, you're not that employable. I'm not saying you should immediately start a blog or a podcast (I mean you can, I have!), but you need to be putting something out there.

In addition to building a following, the series of articles I write and the podcasts I record are interviews. Meaning, they require interviewees. I reach out to a lot of prominent people, both academics and practitioners, directly. Sometimes it goes well, sometimes I get rejected. Oh well. At the very least, they've heard of me. And I get to publish interviews with them, which links me to them, as judged by others. This helps more than you think!

I'm not saying that you need to run out and start a blog and write the days away (especially not if you hate writing…), but this is a way of growing your network, which helps people to find you. You need to make sure you have some type of online presence. At the bare minimum, it helps if you have a fully up-to-date LinkedIn page, as well as a (personal) website which outlines your work, achievements and interests. Just make sure that, in whichever way that suits you, you're out there!

PhD Review, Year 2

As indicated in Chapter 18, the annual reviews of my PhD experience have been copied over directly from their respective blogpost, as to not bias my experience by editing in hindsight.

One of my most popular articles on here [on Money on the Mind] is my review of my first year as a PhD student. As soon as I had written this article, I knew I was going to turn it into a series, because I think it is important to let people know about the honest experience of a PhD, with its many ups and downs. Having said that, here is the second installment: my review of my second year as a PhD student!

Coursework

In the initial article, the first thing I mention is coursework. Well, in the second year, you do not have coursework, unless you make the active choice to audit more courses. People do choose this, but the courses will be rather specialized (such as learning Python, R, and Stata) and will directly apply to their PhD rather than the mismatch of courses we had in our first year. With most of the coursework out of the way, you suddenly have a lot more time over for research. Yes!

Self-reliance and structure

Oh no. Having so much extra time to do more of your actual work seemed like such a great thing. And it does help, and I did feel like I progressed a lot; this came with ups, but also with a lot of downs. Why? Because YOU suddenly have a lot more extra time. But your supervisors and collaborators might not. And after a while, if you get canceled on too often, or double-booked, or just cannot see them often enough, it starts to irk. Because it might mean that suddenly, you have nothing but time on your hands and a problem that is just lying around waiting to be solved. Yikes.

Now I know for a fact I am lucky to see both my supervisors quite regularly. But, we have fallen out as well. Because of aforementioned reasons. When it comes to my own PhD, I do not think of myself as a very self-reliant person, especially not when it comes to the data analysis side of things. I do still need a lot of help when it comes to data analytics. Help can just mean having discussions about measures and outcome variables again, or going through code together because it won't run or doesn't make a lot of sense as is. If you are like me and have clear issues you need help with, you need to figure out, together with your supervisors, how to progress. How often do you need to meet and how often are they available to you? What do you want to do during these meetings? You need a structure to be as efficient as you can be.

Talking about structure, that is gone too. Completely out of the window. With no courses to tie you down, the world is your oyster. You do not need to be on campus, or in the UK even, if you do not want to be, and can work just fine on your own. For some people that is a blessing. For some, that is hell. They spiral between guilt and procrastination and get absolutely no work done, whilst feeling awful about it. If you identify as this type of person, I suggest you artificially try imposing structure on your PhD. One way of doing this is teaching.

Teaching

Most PhDs will try to teach. It is a good experience, it is paid (that PhD wage really is not going to make you rich…), it gives structure and takes away time from research. After reading the part on structure and self-reliance, I hope that me judging the latter as positive no longer surprises you.

I have written articles about my teaching experience, so I will not go too in-depth here. Would I recommend teaching? Yes. Would I recommend you teach every term? No.

Teaching in itself is very draining and takes up more time than just the hours taught, as many will know. I am not just talking about the time invested in preparation. What I mean is that if you prepare for 1 hour and teach for 4 hours, there are effectively 3 more hours left in the working day. I can promise you, you will not be able to produce anything worthwhile in those 3 hours. You are fried. Every day that you have to teach is a complete write-off with regard to research. As such, I do not recommend always teaching a lot. I taught two courses in term 1 that went on for the whole term (meaning my Mondays and Wednesdays were gone). I taught nothing in term 2 and only taught a week-long course in term 3 (I lost just under a week there as we were assisting and helping out rather than actively teaching). I did enjoy it, I will teach again in my third year of the PhD but I do warn against taking on too much teaching. I know for some people it really helps out financially, but you do have to give up energy and time for research to do it. Up to you how you make the trade-off.

Research

As this is the second year, it was time to focus on my actual research rather than just coursework. You are probably wondering why I put this rather late in the article. Well, there is a reason for that. If you read through my blogs, especially the ones about the PhD, you can get a feel for how the research is going anyway. Sometimes I am doing well, sometimes I am annoyed at how slow everything is going and sometimes I just do not want to think about R anymore.

So far, I have managed to write up my first study, which is now in chapter form. I submitted it to a paper and got desk-rejected within 3 days, which was surprisingly fast (still sucked though). I am doing the data analysis for the second project. We have figured out what we want from it and are coding it out after much data cleaning. I hope to have this project in a draft state by December. The third project will be based on the same data and we have a concept for it. Depending on what we find, we will complement the second and third projects with experiments, but we will see how feasible that is with regard to time. So, my research in itself seems to be progressing.

The reason I put research rather late in this article is because you cannot escape having to do it. How you go about doing your research, which methods you need to employ and what timeframe works for you, those are such individualistic aspects of the PhD that they are rather difficult to correctly target in one article. As such, I tend to focus on more general tendencies, such as things I experienced in my second year and have noticed others experienced as well.

Mental health and distractions

I think I might have mentioned the word "structure" about 60 times already, but bear with, because structure (61) is what keeps a lot of people sane. And that is quite nice.

In the second year, what you see is that people, next to their research, do other things. I am not talking about things that are seamlessly related to their PhD, such as teaching, but things that are quite outside of that scope. I myself blog (you might have noticed) and manage the Warwick Behavioural Insights Team. But I know that some take an even more extreme approach and still take on consultancy projects next to the PhD (they do have a background/work experience in consultancy).

I am not telling you this because I think just doing your PhD research is not impressive enough. Or makes you less than. I just think it helps widening your focus, which can be a welcome change. If the only thing you do is your research and you are stuck, you will feel awful. If you have other things next to your own research, you can re-direct your time, and at least feel productive and useful in another aspect of your life. This does not even have to be study or work related. Sports, arts, leading/participating in organizations or charity will do just as well.

If you prefer to stay within your scope, but do need a distraction that does not involve R, how about a conference? You're going to need to attend them anyway, so why not start in your first or second year already? Why wait until you need a job? Conferences provide you with many people who are in your field and topic or at least somewhat adjacent. You can meet people who otherwise you might never have met. It can lead to interesting conversations, interesting contacts and even interesting opportunities if you do it (the networking game that is) right. If you attend because you are speaking yourself, you can improve your presentation skills and put your own research out there.

Now, this might not seem like much of a break; presenting your research and networking within your research area are very tiresome activities. But they are different. And, keep in mind, most conferences require travel. And if you do your research well (and get a bit lucky), you can travel to really nice locations! Maybe even home if you want to (several conferences this year were in Amsterdam, and I was quite pleased)!

Whatever you decide to do, it is good to distract your mind from research that is known to have ups, and downs. No one wants to continuously feel like a failure only because your research is not going well that week. That really will just throw your mental health out of balance. There is more to life than research. Balance (and structure!!!) are key.

Overall, the second year was a year in which I had to re-develop my structure, figured out what it was like to teach and have really enjoyed it. It was also the year in which I finished a chapter and managed to plan out all the others, giving myself a great sense of relief. But, prior to this relief were weeks of banging my head against the wall, useless supervisory meetings and a mental health that was on the decline. It took some time for me to realize what was going on and indicate to my supervisors that this way of working just was not working. And that is fine. Another year, another lesson learned.

PhD Review, Year 3

As indicated in Chapter 18, the annual reviews of my PhD experience have been copied over directly from their respective blogpost, as to not bias my experience by editing in hindsight.

It has become tradition on this blog [Money on the Mind] for me to reflect on each part of the PhD process. As my third year in the PhD comes to an end and I am entering my fourth and final year, it is time to reflect on my third year. Which is exactly what I'll be doing here. I try to describe my experiences as best as I can, so you can get a real grasp of what different parts of the PhD are like. I have written a review for both my first and second years in the PhD as well. Please do read those if you want to have an even better overview!

Term 1

Where to start reviewing the third year? Maybe it's best if we contrast it to the previous year. I don't know if you were able to tell from my review of the second year, but it wasn't my best. By a long way. My second year was terrible, with loads of misunderstandings, slowdowns and disappointments. My supervisors and I figured out we hadn't been on the same page for a while, and the whole process needed a reboot, which happened in the end. Most of the third term of the second year was spent trying to re-figure things out and get the second chapter on the rails.

The third year as a result felt like a completely different year altogether. Weekly meetings were back on track and in the first term I helped out teaching again (Business Statistics). Work was fine, definitely manageable. I was still doing the initial data analysis for the second chapter and I had resubmitted my first chapter (in paper form), as it had been rejected from a different journal quite quickly. This type of rejection might not seem very positive, but rather a quick rejection than one that drags on forever and requires even more work without result.

In addition to this, I also started to think about what my third paper (or chapter) should be. I started to have some ideas, for both myself and collaborations with others. So all in all, not a bad term.

Term 2

It was in term 2 that things really started picking up. I had presented my second chapter (to the extent that it was ready) to the department and had gotten feedback which was effectively along the lines of: "you're doing the wrong analysis, it makes no sense, run this one instead". It took me several hours to recover from that, but after that, my supervisors and I just went for it. We re-ran a completely different analysis and it worked much better. And it was also 10 times easier to explain. As of writing this part of the article (26th of May, 2020) that chapter has been written up. At least its first draft is. I'm sure it will require a lot of edits and finetuning, especially when needing to be submitted to journals, but its core is done, and that's a massive relief.

In term 2, it also became clear that I had gotten a revise and resubmit from the second journal I had submitted my first paper to. This revision requires me to run another study, providing a stronger causal explanation for my findings, which is totally fine. The ethics and funding applications for that study went well and both outcomes were positive. You should have seen me in this second term, I was like a steam roller: couldn't stop me!

Besides being really motivated and getting a lot of work done quite quickly, I also (finally) was able to help teach Neuroeconomics, a course that I really wanted to help teach as I enjoyed taking it a lot when I was in the MSc Behavioural and Economic Science. It was a great experience and good fun!

And then, as the second term came to an end in the first week of March, we entered lockdown. Which is where we still are today (as of the 26th of May).

Term 3

The other shoe needs to drop. Our third term spans the end of April to July. Early March it became clear that COVID-19 wasn't something to be taken lightly, at all. Everything shut down, and I traveled home as soon as I could.

That is exactly where we are today, working from home, which for me is the Netherlands. I'm sure it has been quite an adjustment for everyone, but I can't complain at all. Work hasn't actually been less productive nor have my supervisors been slacking, despite both having children they now have to home-school. Work continues to be productive.

The new and improved analysis for Chapter 2 also provided the foundation for the first part of Chapter 3. Within Chapter 2, we found that one independent variable kept making an appearance, despite the literature not predicting that it should. Well, there's plenty of room for discovery there. The initial data analysis part of chapter three is also already done as I'm writing this, so it'll soon be time to set up an experiment complementing it. So far so good!

The conference season hasn't slowed done either. I have managed to attend plenty of online conferences and will continue to do so throughout this term and probably also year 4. Is it bad that I actually find online conferences much more convenient?

On top of living my best online life, my friend Sarah and I have also started a podcast together. When she proposed the idea my initial reaction was: "Are you mental? Who is going to listen to us blab on?!" Despite my initial doubts and complete lack of technical understanding, it has been a really cool process, and the podcast is doing well. So honestly, I can't really complain. Do give it a listen and let me know what you think!

The only drawback I've really experienced is the inability to conduct real-life experiments. The experiment for Chapter 3 was planned to be fully done online anyway, so it didn't suffer. The additional experiment for Chapter 1 has been postponed, likely to run at the start of the next academic year, if possible. This also postpones the ability to publish the paper, but I think this hardly warrants me complaining…

Overall, the third term has been one hell of a term, probably the best one I've had so far, as weird as it sounds. I think it might have been the reboot by COVID-19 that gave me the space to breathe and figure it all out from scratch. It was that type of break that I needed. I'm not happy with the form it took, as it's wreaking havoc on the world, but it's given me something I seemed to need with regard to personal growth. Silver lining anyone?

Summer term

Did I mention the other shoe had to drop earlier? Well, it did. This part of the article is actually written 3 months later (27th August).

Everything slows down in summer, whether you want it to or not. And I didn't want it to (yes I have an unhealthy relationship with my work, I'm working on that…). "Issue" is, my supervisors have healthy relationships with their work, and families who also need (and deserve) their attention. So, they massively slowed down on the workload, and I was left with more questions rather than actionable guidelines. Lucky thing is I started picking up collaborations with people who aren't my supervisors (this is a good idea!).

However, one collaboration (project 4) is very similar to my second project, and what happened was that my collaborator quite quickly figured out some of the variables had some odd distributions. So that took a while to solve. And in the end, these two projects (2 and 4), due to similarity in analysis, might get merged. I'm still not sure how I feel about that.

I have started collaborating with an industry partner as well, under the supervision of an external academic, together with my supervisors. Let's call this project 5. At the pace this is currently going, I wouldn't be surprised if it's going to take at least another year, but it might qualify as "postdoc stuff".

Projects 6 and 7, with yet another external academic who used to be a professor in my MSc, are in different stages. Project 6 is most definitely her project but needs guidance and some finetuning, and project 7 is actually going to be based on this blog! So that's all exciting stuff!

All in all, I got frustrated quite a bit, but managed to turn my (unwarranted) frustration from being "held back" by my supervisors who were on their break into other collaborations. Which is good. It's healthy!

Last, I designed (with loads of help from a kind stranger from Twitter) the experiment for my third project, which should be able to run somewhere in late September. So that's pretty good!

Plans for year 4

You might have noticed that I'm pretty close to satisficing the three-paper criterium set by the WBS PhD guidelines. So what does year 4 hold?

Well, as I said before, project 1 still needs an additional experiment, which will have to be run online. I hope to have that all sorted out before November. Project 2 requires some proper exclusion criteria for variable levels, but the analyses themselves are sound. Project 3, because it's based on a similar analysis as project 2, will be recoded as well, and the additional experiment will be run in September. For the thesis itself, I'm probably keeping project 4 as its own chapter. My collaborator knows this and is fine with it. The topic of this research is mobile payments rather than contactless payments, which is why the analysis is quite similar (it also comes from the same data). For publication purposes, it might be that projects 2 and 4 merge into one paper. Which is fine.

Having mentioned postdocs in the summer term section, my fourth year will focus on applying to postdocs in general. To be more attractive for those positions, it's quite important to have published work, so most of my time and energy will go into journal submissions. Wish me luck!

You might also have noticed I haven't mentioned anything about teaching. I'm not planning to teach at all during my final year. At least, not for the 10-week courses. Of course, I will continue to write here. I have no intentions of bailing on you, my dear reader!

The third year summarized

I think it's safe to say that my third year was my best year so far. Much less problems, 10 times more motivation and despite COVID-19, a better working environment. And it shows. I got a lot more done and also feel in a much better position. I'm ready for the fourth and final year. Let's do it!

If you want to know more about my PhD experience, I have written a review for both my first and second years in the PhD as well. Please do read those if you had any more questions about doing a PhD.

36

Concluding Remarks

We covered a lot of ground in this section. I've taken you from the amazing things that the PhD can offer you: teaching, conferences, a growing network and working together with amazing people on a multitude of projects that you find interesting. At the same time, I've outlined some issues you might want to take into account, such as the lack of structure, time management, the pressure and timelines of publishing, supervisor communications and knowing what you actually want out of a PhD. Last, I've outlined the worst possible scenarios in terms of breakdowns in mental health, supervisor communications, where and how to find support and general reasons to consider pausing or even quitting the PhD.

Like I said, we went through a lot!

It is difficult to conclude such a myriad of topics. Neatly summarizing them is far beyond my abilities, which is ironic, given that I've written them. The only advice I can give in addition to the 16 (!!!) chapters we've just gone through is to check in with yourself, constantly. How are you feeling? What are you thinking? How are you experiencing all the things going on in your PhD? And in your life in general? You'll need this type of introspection to find out whether the PhD is really for you; whether research makes you happy; whether you and your supervisor actually get along and can continue to have a fruitful relationship or at least a healthy collaborative effort; and last, what it is you actually want from the PhD, and what you need to achieve that.

From my perspective, the chapters on mental health and failure were the hardest to write. Mental health issues, as I've reiterated many times already, are incredibly prominent in academia, especially in the lower ranks (PhD, post-doc, essentially before tenure!). Make sure you build yourself a support network before it gets too bad. Before therapy is the only option left. And make sure to always, and I do mean always, keep perspective. You are not "a PhD student". The PhD is not your entire goal, focus or identity. You are a human being currently enrolled in a PhD program, doing research. It's something you do, not something you are. These are two very different things psychologically, trust me.

In addition to having an identity that spans beyond the PhD, make sure you actually have a life next to it. Have friends, other hobbies, events to go to that aren't work related, sports, baking competitions or go fishing (literally) for all I care. Have other areas in your life from which you can derive you, or maybe even reward. It will make all the difference and it does help with perspective keeping. It may be 4* years of your life, and it may feel like forever once you're in it. But in the grand scheme of things, it's only 4* years of your life.

Hopefully, you can use the time during your PhD to gain some great experience and experiences. If possible, travel to amazing places for amazing conferences (the global situation permitting). Go on research visits. Get to know different universities, departments and research groups and get a good idea of what academia is like, or could be like, for you. Use the time to learn new skills, skills that can help you for the rest of your life, whether you decide to spend it in academia, industry, or both!

Make sure to take the PhD experience and make it what you want it to be. There will be obstacles, but you are there to learn, and don't forget: a PhD is training you to become an independent researcher. You're not there yet, and there's still lots to learn! There are also a lot of freedoms in the PhD, for better or for worse. I hope this book can make sure it's for the better.

---

*It could be longer or shorter, depending on the program, field, country, etc. I got tired of using numerical ranges.

Section 5

Finishing the PhD

The end is nigh. The end is nigh! Congratulations on making it this far — it's genuinely impressive — but we're not done yet!

The end of the PhD might be the hardest part. There's light at the end of the tunnel, but the tunnel isn't finished yet. It's time to collect all the remaining resolve you still have, and you hopefully still have some, and put it to work. This is the final stretch.

And I'm making it sound like an epic heroic novel because it is. Not only do you have to finish the PhD but also you'll have to prepare for your next step(s) as well. What are you going to do after the PhD? Just because the time isn't upon us yet, doesn't mean you don't have to prepare for it. And this will take up time.

At the same time that your workload is increasing or possibly "just" diversifying, you'll start to see the effects of longer-term stress, as well as having ponders about the true value of holding a PhD now that you've done it. This may be both excruciating and exhilarating. It can go either way to be honest.

It's also possible that finally, after years of hard work, it dawns on you that there is now very limited time to still reach some of the goals you had set yourself in the PhD. It's possible, and quite likely, that you're rushing towards the end, getting it all done. People react very differently to short periods of time being left, compared to years and years being left. So prepare for that too!

Whichever way it may go for you, I'll do my best to describe these possibilities in detail in the upcoming chapters. It's time to finish this PhD!

Balancing the PhD with the Job Hunt

In previous chapters, I outlined the importance of being able to multi-task, or at least, manage different projects at the same time and, also, making sure (parts of) those are written up. Why? Well, because towards the end of the PhD, you'll be doing a lot of writing still: you'll be writing job applications. And they take time…

Now if you've been compliant with this book and its advice, you'll have built yourself a nice network. A network in which, now that the end is in sight, you can drop the message that you're going to be graduating soon and are looking for jobs. In academia, this should be approximately 6–12 months in advance, leaning more towards 12 months. In industry, the timeline is very different and is more like 3–5 months, supposing that you want to start immediately after the PhD or with only a short break in between.

In addition to simply dropping a message on your social media, you can also directly send out emails and see where this takes you. Maybe they have job openings for you or can direct you to colleagues or co-workers who do. This is one of the many advantages of having a network: you increase your chances of being hired by having access to more of this type of "insider" information. And that can make all the difference.

If this is essentially the path you're working with, I doubt you'll be shooting out a lot of job applications. If you start early enough and the positions you're interested in are actually available, you can do several applications simultaneously or even sequentially: waiting to hear back from one before doing the next, so as to minimize the time spent on this process. If this works for you and you get a job offer early on, that's great!

However, as I've mentioned before, a lot of PhD students aren't that fortunate. Whether you start early, have a great network and had planned out exactly where to go, things can still go wrong. Until a contract is signed, you're still not employed anywhere. Especially if plans fall through, for whatever reason, you can still find yourself with nothing.

It's also possible if you've only recently decided that you want to stay in academia or want to move to industry. If you decide this relatively late, you may not have the network to support this decision.

Regardless of what may or may not be applicable to you, a lot of PhD students find themselves applying to a lot of different positions, both in industry and academia. And when it becomes a numbers game, and you have to send out more than 100 job applications, you're suddenly looking at another full-time job.

Given the time job applications can take up, it's important that you manage your time even better towards the end of the PhD. This is also why I urge you to manage your projects well at the start of your PhD and build yourself a structure which accounts for this time as well. If you can juggle multiple projects at different stages of completion throughout the PhD, the chances of having one (or more) finished or close to completion at the end of your PhD are much higher, meaning that the time which was initially spent on one of these research projects can now be directed towards job applications. If you have multiple projects close to completion or even completed (and submitted), you can direct even more time to your applications. And more time means more applications or higher quality applications.

This is also the reason why I don't recommend you leave writing until the very end of the PhD. What happens in this case is that you'll be writing up PhD research from several years ago (which is very time consuming), then have to write this up in a cohesive manner to fit the PhD dissertation as a whole, and when that's done, your other task is to write job applications. I love writing, but even I find that too much writing does not motivate me. If you don't even like writing, this is not going to be a fun process for you.

I'm not saying job application writing will ever be fun, but at least it shouldn't be complete torture...

But what if you don't have this time available? What if all of your projects are still at different stages of completion and require a lot more work to be completed? Or your one project still requires a lot of (full-time) work? Or, unfortunately, time was mismanaged and a lot of writing still remains to be done, squashing the time you have for job applications? Well, this is where the misery begins.

I believe in structure, I really do. I manage my time in an excel sheet in which every day is split by the hour, and most activities are color coded. This works for me. If your current system isn't really working for you, try this one. Now I hope you've built yourself a type of working calendar before. I'd be surprised if you've made it this far into the PhD working willy-nilly, but it is of course possible. So let's assume that by now, you at least know your most productive working hours, or have some semblance of structure and stability in your working week. Knowing this, where can you fit more work? Where can you cut corners?

I don't mean cutting corners in the quality of your PhD research. I mean it in time spent. Sometimes we plan things rather leisurely: we set aside an entire day for a task which, if we really pulled ourselves together, could be done in four hours. I recommend you start looking very critically at your time allocations. Every hour you can save and direct towards job applications is an additional application done. Assuming you have the documents ready.

Also, I can imagine that you might be wondering where you're supposed to find these hundreds of jobs. Depending on the country and field you're in, there'll be job sites for your specific field of interest. Your colleagues and supervisors should know what they are and can direct you. There'll also be mailing lists for organizations in your field, it's smart to subscribe to those as well. Make sure you're tapped into every stream of information regarding potential jobs.

There'll be start-up costs to getting the right documents ready for job applications. First point is to know which documents are needed, on average, for the types of jobs you're applying to. Academic applications (postdocs, fellowships, assistant professorships) require, at a minimum, a CV, motivation letter, references and a writing sample (PhD chapter/paper). It is also possible they require more documents, such as a research statement, teaching statement, diversity statement, a cover letter, transcripts, previous degrees, more writing samples or proof of work done beyond the PhD (more industry-focused work, science communications, etc.).

It pays to have the bare minimum in documents ready from the get-go. My advice here is to simply take out a day, and yes, it might have to be a weekend day, to bang those documents out. Google what an academic CV should look like, edit yours to fit the mold (there are programmes for that too) and send it off to get checked by your supervisors, mentors or colleagues. Your writing sample, which you should largely have ready as this is key to your PhD, can also be sent out to be checked. At the same time that you're sending these documents out, ask supervisors and mentors whether they're happy being your references. They are prepared for having to write those, you're not going to be the first to ask them, trust me.

The motivation letter is a bit trickier. Although it is a minimum requirement document, it changes per job applied for, as this letter needs to outline your experience, interests and why you want this specific job. As a result, you'll need different versions for each and every job, because you'll have to tailor your interests and motivation to the job at hand. I do think it pays to have a more general version of the motivation letter, in which you can edit specific sections to fit the job you're applying for, rather than rewriting the whole thing again. However, this only really works when you're applying to jobs in the same niche, sector or field. If you're really aiming for a much wider variety of jobs, you may need a variety of "base" motivation letters as well. And this will cost more time. Also, make sure to get these motivation letters checked as well!

So getting the minimum requirements ready should take you approximately one day, which is just a day you need to take out of your schedule and dedicate to this process. If it takes you two days rather than one, well, that's a weekend gone I'm afraid.

After you've got the minimum requirements done, you'll need to look at which jobs are available (it's quite likely that your first, "base", motivation letter was written with a specific job in mind) and start the applications for them. Upload your documents, see which other documents are required (if any) and make those as well. Edit the motivation letter if required (it needs to be a different version per job!) and Bob is your auntie. I think once you've got the hang of them, most applications will take about an hour.

But where are you going to find these hours? I've already mentioned that some PhD students will have to send out more than 100 job applications. That's 100 hours, not counting the initial document prep. That's

2.5 weeks of work. If you're rushing towards the end, this might be a bit much.

I have to admit that often, the last part of a PhD isn't particularly nice. It can be very stressful. The way to deal with this additional time management constraint is to figure out what works for you. Do you prefer to bang out a job application each day before you start your PhD work? Or immediately after? Or during, say, around the lunchtime period? Or, if that's really not feasible, do you dedicate an entire day to nothing but job applications, at the expense of the PhD research? Or not at the expense of the PhD research, but during the weekend? Is that something that you can maintain for a longer time?

After shooting out a lot of applications, it's not uncommon to not hear anything back for a long while, or not at all. If you do hear back that's great, but chances are it's a rejection (statistically more likely. It's not you, it's the system). If you do move to the next round the interviews start.

The interviews will be scheduled in a way which is convenient for them, not you. During the pandemic, these interviews were done online, but often these interviews occur face to face, meaning that if you have to fly over there (called a fly-out), you'll lose much more time. In addition to the interview, they may also ask you to prepare a presentation on your PhD research and even prepare a seminar or lecture (or a 10-minute version of this), to showcase your teaching abilities. This all takes up time, and you need to take this into account. We're no longer talking hours, we're talking days and weeks. So make sure that your projects are in stages of completion when this process starts. And don't underestimate it!

So far, I've only described academic job applications. The reason for this is simple: they come first, and they're much more document heavy. Some of you will apply for academic positions when you're 6–12 months away from submitting, and some of you won't. Some of you will exclusively apply to industry positions, and some of you will apply to both.

Industry applications require different documents. They require your CV but tailored to industry (there's a difference, make sure you have an industry-oriented academic or an industry partner look yours over!). Industry CVs tend to be shorter and more experience oriented. They require summaries rather than extensive descriptions, and they often have a focus on your skillset: what skills did the PhD teach you rather than its exact topic.

Beyond your CV, industry applications may require a cover letter, which is the same as the motivation letter in academia. Again, you'll have to edit this one to fit the job at hand.

Often, these two documents are for round one. It's possible that you also have to upload your degrees or transcripts, but this doesn't occur frequently. As a result, the industry application process is quicker. At least, at the start.

If you go through to the next round, they may require more documents that are seemingly more tailored. However, the more likely scenario is that you'll be invited to an interview or a case study (form of assessment). If you're invited to do a case study, you'll be sent a problem statement that'll require a solution. There'll be guidelines to what that solution should look like and how it should be presented to the company you're applying for. This is a process which can also easily take a weekend. So if you do multiple applications like this, you won't have much free time, if any, left.

After the assessment, if you move onto the next round, there'll be one or more interviews. It's also possible that one of these interviews is also an assessment. Depending on your field and industry of choice, there may be written assessments, coding assessments, presentation assessments, etc.

At the end of this process, it'll have taken as much time as the academic job applications. It's just that industry is a bit lighter on documents, but much heavier on interviews.

I've tried outlining the steps of the different job applications, to paint you a picture of how time consuming this process can be. If this becomes a numbers game, for whatever reason, keep in mind that you'll have to dedicate significant amounts of time to this process. It's not for the fainthearted, especially not as it comes with a lot of rejection. Something we'll discuss again in Chapter 39. But first, we'll go to Chapter 38, in which I'll discuss ways in trying to prevent you from entering this numbers game, by getting a job earlier on, through leveraging your contacts.

38
Leveraging Contacts

As you will have gathered from the previous chapter, job applications can be quite the madness, and it's advisable to avoid the numbers game to the best of your abilities.

In previous chapters, I've outlined the how and why of building up a network. I hope you read those chapters carefully because we're going to discuss the advantages of having a network and how to leverage that network here.

For academia, I'm hoping that you've had conferences, collaborations and visits with other people, groups and institutions. Or, at least, that you've met and gotten to know lots of people in your field, and they know you and your research as well.

Now, rather obvious, your main contact to leverage is your supervisor(s). They should know about opportunities arising in their own network and should be able to pass these onto you. They may even have some insider information, knowing about jobs that are available before they even get advertised, through their own collaborative network. This can be very helpful. Do discuss your career plans with your supervisor(s) and see how much they're willing to help you and what they can do for you.

In addition to your supervisor(s), your mentor, if you have one, should be able to help you as well, for similar reasons. If they're a field-specific mentor, they should also have insight into the current market, and through their network, be able to (help you) identify jobs that fit your profile.

Worst-case scenario, both your supervisor(s) and mentor(s) should be able to provide you with great references.

Going back to the conferences, collaborations and visits, if there's one thing the pandemic taught me, it's that everyone's just an email away. If you have certain key players in your network (research group leads, prominent academics, researchers who just received grants, etc.), make sure to reach out to them to see if they'd consider taking you on. Even if they can't take you on, they may be able to point you in the direction of someone who can. If you're recommended by someone, you're also 1–0 ahead of the game!

In general, the advice here is to do a lot of the leg work in advance: go to conferences, meet people, set up research collaborations and do research visits. Get to know multiple research groups and institutions that may be of interest to you to pursue a post-doc (or equivalent) in. The world is your oyster, but you do need to crack it.

For industry, the advice is not too different. Again, the leg work came before. I'm hoping you went to industry-based conferences and events beforehand, that you set up collaborations or data sharing agreements and have shown those collaborators what you can do, or that you did some (consultancy type) work for some companies in general. This should definitely give you a leg up, as you've already proven to be an asset to the company.

Talking about assets, everyone in your network is an asset, so use them. Reach out to key industry players (CEOs, research unit managers, team leads, etc.) to re-introduce yourself and mention that you're going to be available for work soon. Maybe your industry contact is not a key player but can put in a good word for you. Again, it's time to get cracking!

I hope I reiterated the importance of doing a lot of leg work during the start and midsection of the PhD to build yourself a healthy network. It can really help get your name out there, and increase your chances of getting hired early on, or at least earlier on, which can help you avoid the numbers game described in the previous chapter.

The reason I'm so keen for you to avoid it is that it really takes up a lot of time. Time that is better spent on your PhD research. The number of rejections associated with the numbers game is also no joke. And as we've learned in Chapter 27, rejections can really mess up your mental health. More on that in the next chapter.

39
Mental Health Revisited

You might be wondering why there's another mental health chapter in this section of the book, as we've already discussed mental health, in Chapter 27. I've already described how a lack of structure, constant (negative) feedback and social comparison can exponentially decrease your wellbeing and how to prevent or deal with it when it occurs.

However, that chapter focused exclusively on the PhD itself. When approaching the end of the PhD, several other factors also start to come into play. As described in Chapters 37 and 38, you'll be facing much more immediate deadlines, planning for the future and doing job applications that could potentially take up a lot of time. And in addition to these job applications taking up a lot of time, there's a high chance of rejection too. Rejection is essentially a form of negative feedback, but it's feedback of a completely different type, pertaining to a very different aspect of your life. And that can hit differently.

Towards the end of the PhD, things start shifting. The end is in sight, and deadlines which once seemed far away are now uncomfortably close. Close deadlines can have the effect of sending people into a spiraling panic, in which they realize how much work they still have to do in very little time. If that's you, prepare for this. Also prepare for the fact that your supervisor(s) might not have a similar reaction to you at all, because to them the deadline is much more artificial: a lot of these projects can be continued after submission for them. This is especially likely if you are staying in academia, and/or these projects are collaborative efforts.

When you feel like you're starting to spiral, make sure you take a couple of deep breaths, tell your supervisor(s) and plan accordingly. What I mean with "plan accordingly" is figure out what still needs doing and actually plan it in on a week-to-week basis, if you're several months away from submission, or maybe even a day-to-day basis, if you're weeks away from submission. This planning will show you what is feasible and what isn't, and that which is feasible needs to be done by a certain date. This can be a big relief to some people. Having a plan can have that effect.

You might also want to indicate to your supervisor(s) that you're going to need more support towards the end, if they hadn't caught onto that themselves. This support can take many forms: it can be longer or more frequent meetings or them spending the hours checking your work. Whatever works for you.

It is likely that this panic spiral, if unresolved, will result in increased working hours. Most people towards the end of the PhD, especially the last 3 months, are not doing 40 hours. You could continue to work 40 hours if you have been excellent at planning and sticking to the planning throughout the PhD (by following all the advice in this book, for example, …), but that doesn't seem to happen for most people. What does happen is that people "go hard" on the last mile. As I've said before, I'm not a massive fan of working way beyond your capacity for long(er) periods of time, but this often isn't a long(er) period of time, this is the short finale sprint. So if that's what works for you, or you simply have to do it, then I wish you the best of luck!

Described above is the healthy scenario: you know you need to put extra hours in, you've got your plan and your supervisor's support, and you're going for it. However, that's not really the most common result of the spiral. The result of the spiral is panic working, which is a form of working in which you work excessive hours, and you panic when you're not working, which will affect your periods of rest, often leading to diminished sleep and as a result, increased stress and decreased cognitive ability.

My solutions to this are similar to those in Chapter 27, you need to let people know. Tell your supervisors so they can help you (by increased support, or the making of the work plan, or both). Tell your support networks (friends, family and cohort colleagues). Tell your mentor so they can talk you through their experience. And if it's really taking on abnormal proportions, you need to talk to a professional, such as a counselor or therapist.

Panic working became a recognized mental health term during the initial wave of remote work during the pandemic. People were scared of losing their jobs and thought they could prove to their boss how much of an asset they were to the team by increasing their output. Add this to the fact that remote working doesn't offer real boundaries for when you work, and when you don't, and you have yourself a pressure cooker in which people are working constantly, out of fear. This is an actual thing, so don't think that no one will understand what you're going through or that no one can help you. Panic working often lays at the forefront of a burnout, so this will, and should, be taken seriously!

Another aspect of mental health which warrants discussing is how it's going to be impacted by the increased negative feedback you're likely to receive.

If you heeded my advice and had your colleagues and supervisor(s) read and edit your work throughout the PhD, the negative feedback coming from this endeavor should be known to you already. Essentially, you should've become accustomed to it already. If you did not heed my advice, and you waited till the final year of your PhD to let anyone read your work, prepare yourself for some serious feedback. I remember sending my first draft of my first study to my supervisors. It came back with more red text than black text and had approximately 25+ comments per A4 page. Do you now understand why I don't think leaving this until the end is a good idea?! So my advice here: have people read your work throughout and write throughout!

Regardless of whether you've grown numb to negative feedback on your work, what you'll likely have a lot less experience with is with being rejected for a large number of jobs (the average PhD student hasn't yet been rejected for tens or hundreds of different job applications). And this can hit hard.

Being rejected over and over again, whereas people around you may have secured job offers, or are receiving less rejections, is very difficult. I would even call it painful. Again, (social) comparison is the thief of all joy, but in this case, it goes a lot deeper than that. If you're starting to develop extreme negative thoughts that are bordering on being incessant, you need help. It's completely natural that constant negative feedback makes you feel awful, but feeling awful every so often as a direct result of a negative comment is still very far removed from feeling like you're a failure, constantly.

Depression is very common amongst those in the lower ranks of academia, and needs to be dealt with, or managed, professionally. Don't worry about having to admit to yourself or others that you have depression. It's not a character flaw, it's a chemical imbalance in the brain. It can happen to anyone.

Let's now take a bird's eye view of the context and resulting mental state of the average PhD student. It's likely that the increased stress, or possibly full-blown panic working, can only be maintained by an increased motivation to finish the PhD. However, if you're receiving constant negative feedback (comments on your work, rejections from jobs) at the same time, harboring a high level of motivation is near impossible.

This is when working from motivation has to make way for working from discipline. Motivation is, unfortunately, a rather fickle resource. Discipline on the other hand is not. Now, I'm not saying that you have to work 12 hours per day, until you're simply in tears at the end of the week and going to bed crying every night. I'm just saying that if you have made a plan with your supervisor to make sure that you can finish your PhD dissertation on time, you cannot deviate from this plan.

This may seem rather contradictory to my advice in all the previous chapters on mental health and taking breaks, where I mention that if you think you need a "mental health day off" you should take it. Yes, it's important to rest. Yes, it's important to recharge. And yes, you should take care of your mental health. But in the very end of a PhD, and I mean the last month or so, not the last half year, the priority is to finish the PhD. Everything else will likely have to be moved to the back burner for a bit. Again, this is only for a month or so, and if you feel like you need the final sprint! If you don't feel like you need to sprint the last mile, well, then don't.

The advice I give in this chapter is different from the advice in Chapter 27. And that's simply because the timelines are different. You should not be overworking in year 2, being several years removed from submission. You should have a support system and other things next to the PhD during all of the PhD, even the latter period. You should have hobbies too, and other areas in your life from which you can derive a sense of self, a sense of achievement, and your identity and self-worth. However, as with every aspect of life, sometimes one part just needs more attention for a while. You'll need to grind away at one specific aspect to get it to a level where you're happy with it. And in the last month or so of the PhD, everything else will have to move for the PhD. Unless you're not an anxious person and have been working on discipline and impeccable planning this whole time. In that case, this chapter was not for you at all. Impressive!

It's also possible that, despite knowing that the end will be intense and despite you having prepared yourself for this, you're simply not coping. If that's the case you can ask for an extension. Your supervisor(s) and department will be able to tell you what the options are in terms of extensions, their duration and their financial repercussions. Some extensions can be paid for; most of them aren't unless there's good reason for them being paid for (like a pandemic!). In addition, there might be funding options such as additional teaching or additional grants that you can apply for to support yourself throughout the extensions. But this warrants further conversation with your supervisor(s), department or research group. But it is possible.

I'm raising this option as it is, in fact, an option. However, I do strongly urge you to only extend your PhD if you're really not able to finish the dissertation in any way. This can be because of mental health reasons as mentioned above or because of issues with the research itself (delay in data delivery, issues with methodology and further testing needed) or a massive change in circumstance (again, pandemic). The issue with a PhD dissertation, or research of any kind, is that the owner of it will never think it's finished. You'll never think it's perfect or ready for submission. But I'm here to remind you, that the best PhD is a finished PhD! So make sure you decide what needs to be done additionally before even applying for an extension before you're stuck "perfecting" the PhD dissertation forever. Let's discuss that in turn.

A Good PhD Is a Finished PhD

Asking for an extension on the submission deadline of a PhD seems fair if something beyond your control has occurred. Research is a risky business, and predictions are no one's forte.

As I've outlined in previous chapters, there can be very good reasons to pause the PhD, or, if you're towards the end, asking for more time in the form of an extension. Research might have been delayed, some of the processes may have taken more time than initially planned for and you may have had to switch topics, supervisor(s), methodologies or even departments, which is very likely causing delays, making the initial deadline more and more unattainable.

If you can arrange that your department or supervisor(s) funds your extension, that's great. In that case, take the extension and get done what you need to get done (I'd strongly recommend planning this out with your supervisor(s)). However, make sure that there is a clear end goal to this extension too, and stick to it. Because I've seen people get extension after extension, and that's just not the way to go about it.

It's also possible you're in a very different system from the one I'm describing above. In the UK PhD system, you have a set deadline from the moment you enrolled in the program. That deadline is set in stone: as soon as that date has passed, you're out of funding (unless you've applied for more or have arranged an extension). There are systems, most notably in the US, in which there is a "vague" deadline at the end of approximately

5–7 years, however, your supervisor, sometimes also called PI or promotor, can block your submission. If they don't think it's ready, you won't be able to submit.

Now, there's a variety of reasons for why they may do this: (1) they genuinely don't think the work is there yet and needs more, whatever more means, or (2) they want to keep you around as a PhD student for longer, often for not-so-great reasons, such as having cheap labor around. If it's the latter case, go to HR or anyone else high up in the department to make sure you can submit, and get out! If it's the former, you need to sit down with each other and discuss how much more needs to be done for you to submit a thesis they approve of. Depending on all the additional work and edits they require, you can determine how much additional time you're going to need. Also, if they're the ones blocking your submission, make sure that they also help you find additional funding to make this worth your while!

It may be that what you need is not extra time for the research but extra time for yourself. The sprint, as I've described it in the previous chapter, can take it out of you. You do need a certain level of dedication and energy to be able to make it to the finish line. If all of your resources are utterly depleted as a result of mental health issues, this sprint may not be feasible. You could ask for an extension to be able to take a break and recharge your mental health.

But even if it's your mental health at stake, ask yourself this question: what will be better for my mental health: taking a break now and having to come back to it? Or, finishing this thing now and being free from it?

This is not an easy question to answer, and no one answer is better than the other. Some really just need the additional time. Others will think of nothing but finishing the PhD, even during their break, rendering the break rather useless. You might also want to discuss this with others as well. Your support network may be able to give their own views on this (friends, colleagues and mentor(s)), and it would be wise to involve your therapist or counselor as well, if you have one.

Even if none of the above is going on, but you feel like you would be able to hand in a significantly better dissertation if you had three more months, again, communicate this to your supervisor(s), see if they agree, and if so, apply for the extension. But, with a plan. Be very clear about what you want to improve about the dissertation and stick to the deadline.

There'll never be an end to the things you could change, you could edit, you could dive into deeper, "if you only had a little more time". I get it, I really do. But there is a deadline. And remember, just because you've handed the thesis in, doesn't mean your work is done. But more on that in Chapter 45. But let's first actually hand this thing in!

Submission!

The moment we have all been waiting for: submission. Are you ready? Because I wasn't.

It can be a nerve-wracking process. You have checked your document multiple times already. It seems alright. Figures are where they're supposed to be. Footnotes make sense. References are correctly formatted. Okay, everything in your text editor looks good.

Now, we slowly move towards the submission portal. Make sure to attach all the forms! Print, sign, scan and merge with the original document. Does it still look good? Yes, it still looks good. Okay moving on. Upload onto the portal. Check the upload although it couldn't possibly be a different document than the one you've already checked 250 times. Yes, it's the right document. Now submit. Just press the button. Press it. Now please…

When I submitted my dissertation, I was actually giddy with nerves. I sat in the home office nervously giggling behind my laptop screen, at 8 pm on a Monday (the 27th of September, 2021, I'll never forget it), and had to force myself to actually push the button to submit. There was so much dread behind that single push. What if there's still a typo? What if I could've done better? Are they going to fail me?! It makes sense that after years of hard work, and knowing nothing but hard work, the end of it, or something that signals the "end of an era", can be rather frightening. But you'll have to get through it. So push that button and let the feels hit you.

Because there'll be feels. Initially, your heart drops. For a couple of seconds, you'll feel nothing but dread at what you've just done. And then slowly, but surely, relief starts spreading through your entire body. And the relief is followed by triumph. Because you've just submitted your PhD dissertation. Who's the legend? You're the legend!

It's also possible that, unlike the "pandemic cohorts", you also had to hand in a physical copy of your dissertation. The pandemic definitely reduced printing costs and I'm wondering how much longer the tradition of the physical handing in will persist, given the fact that it just seems to be an archaic waste of paper.

Anyway, let's assume you also had to do this, either exclusively, or in addition to the online submission (the latter is more likely). Your department will have an extensive guideline on how, where and what to print. Follow these guidelines to the T. Send off your documents in time, pick them up on time and submit them at the location marked "X", which is very likely the library. This process, from what I've heard, is a lot less nerve-racking as the online submission, because it comes later and quite frankly is a hassle. It's difficult to keep up this level of adrenaline production when a printer is taking a minimum of 5–10 minutes to spew out over 200 pages, which then needed to be bound together, and parts of it even laminated. After that, you may have to sprint across campus to hand it in at the right location. Adrenaline simply doesn't work like that.

And then, *la moment supreme*: you take your big book of wisdom and drop it off where it needs to go. Because this process is a bit more physical than the online submission, you might still have *feels*. The same dread-relief-triumph combo may hit you in this moment. I'd recommend just riding the rollercoaster and celebrating with your friends. Or alone with a good book you've been meaning to read. Or with an all-nighter gaming session. Or having a nice long family call. Whatever floats your boat. It's your submission, so it's your party!

Final-Year PhD Review

As indicated in Chapter 18, the annual reviews of my PhD experience have been copied over directly from their respective blogpost, as to not bias my experience by editing in hindsight.

As always, when a year in the PhD comes to an end, my review of said year emerges. It has become a tradition on this blog for me to reflect on each part of the PhD process. As my fourth and final year in the PhD comes to an end, it is time to reflect on it. Which is exactly what I'll be doing here. I try to describe my experiences as best as I can, so you can get a real grasp of what different parts of the PhD are like. I have written a review for my first and second and third year in the PhD as well. Please do read those if you want to have an even better overview!

I'll be splitting the year into terms, and I'm writing up my experience at the end of each. To break the fourth wall: I started this article on 16/12/2020, as that is around the time the first term ended, and I actually had time to write this up. So let's dive in!

Term 1

Following from a surprisingly excellent and productive third-year summer term, the start to this term seemed promising. We continued to design our skew and our second grocery store experiment, which now are both online. Nothing really new here. We also continued looking at the data analysis for the second project, as we're still stuck on having found a rather large coefficient, that makes rather little sense, for one of our more important dependent variables. This is holding back that project a bit. We found a similar issue within the fourth project, as they are based on the same data, and I'm starting to wonder to what extent you can "explain away" bad data. Yes, I am getting increasingly frustrated with that.

The fifth project, the one with a bank, was moved into the stages of having data shaped up and access being granted, so there is a slow start there. I expect to be able to clean, manipulate and analyze the data towards the end of the second term. Bit late for the PhD, but this could easily flow into a different job, such as a post-doc.

My projects with my Australian collaborator are also moving forward, despite moving rather slowly. Given her intense teaching term and my PhD, and all the other stuff in my life, this was to be expected. Her teaching ended this term, so the winter break and the second term will see a rise in productivity on this front!

Despite initially saying that I wouldn't teach during my final year, I was essentially begged to help out with a module I was used to teaching anyway (Business Statistics), as there was a new module leader on the block, a shortage of TAs and the novelty of online teaching looming over us all. So I did teach this term, which I quite enjoyed. It also gave my week slightly more structure, as structure keeps going out of the window with each new lockdown or tier-of-COVID-panic change. I'm obeying all rules, but let's not pretend it's not as tedious as anything. So the structure was good and so was the course, claps to Tim for being a good module coordinator. It also made me decide to teach again next term (2nd term), as online teaching continues, lockdowns will probably continue, and I need the structure. The additional money is also nice. Online shopping has gotten a bit out of hand…

With regard to job searching, I've been putting the hours in. It's recommended to start looking for post-doc opportunities about a year beforehand. This is with a focus on grant money though and matters especially for the US. Within Europe, you can start 6–8 months before, and Australia seems similar (this is just advice I'd like to get out there). Sometimes you have to apply for both grants and post-doc schemes separately, which is a complete hassle. I haven't been looking at post-docs or academic jobs exclusively. I also looked into industry and I am "leveraging my contacts" (uhuh) but jobs in industry don't want to wait another 10 months for you to finish, their turnover is much quicker. As things stand, I'm leaning towards working in industry more than working in academia. There are several fundamental issues I have with academia that have given rise to many a frustration, which I've aired on the Questioning Behaviour Podcast several times over.

As I'm reflecting back on this term, I have not chosen a great moment to do so, mood-wise. The day before I had a "nice" long chat with one of my supervisors, in which we aired some frustrations with each other. I initially asked for the call after a particularly bad miscommunication, which was "the final drop". Out of this 1.5-hour long chat, we concluded we have very different working styles and different experiences (obviously) and that our communication styles don't match very well either. We also agreed we should have had the call much earlier. In the end, we came up with some practical solutions for dealing with our problems, which was the outcome I wanted. Despite achieving the initial goal (at least we have a verbal understanding), some of the things said cut deep. My self-esteem has taken a massive tumble. Again. The PhD is not for the fainthearted or the insecure…

Term 2

As good as the start was to term 1, as rubbish was the start to term 2. Because of the meeting I had had with my supervisor halfway through December and the things that got said, I decided to just throw myself into my work even more, to start feeling better about myself. So I went from really long intense work weeks, to even longer and more intense work weeks. I barely hung out with my family and did not take an actual break for either Christmas (I took one day off) or New Year's (I again took one day off). Unsurprisingly, this phase didn't last very long, as this is simply not maintainable, and by this stage, I hadn't had a break in close to a year. Additionally, now that I'm back in the UK, I won't be able to fly home to see my family before I finish my PhD, I am thoroughly regretting the fact that I spent so much time working and didn't spend more of it with them.

To get back to the actual PhD side of things, progress was made. For your perspective: I am writing the review of this term on 26/03/2021. After meetings started back up halfway January, my supervisors were happy with my progress and my second and third chapters began to take a form in which only the writing requires editing and not the analysis (sigh of relief). Additionally, we were finally able to finish off the pre-registration for one of my online experiments which I was able to run in less than a day. You cannot imagine my relief and overjoyment when that experiment was run and I could just move onto the analysis of the results.

As soon as I started analyzing those results, however, I ran into the issue that they are non-conforming to previous research in the weirdest possible ways, so now we're trying to figure out what to do here. I will admit very honestly that this is becoming an increasingly larger source of frustration, as neither I nor my supervisors really understand what is going on...

I have so far also not been able to complete my first chapter (the r&r) as there are still too many restrictions due to COVID-19, I am optimistic that we should be able to run this by the end of April. And quite frankly, whether we can or cannot, we will just have to.

On the topic of what is known as my fifth project (with the bank), the data have been received and progress is being made. I have no idea whether this will fit into the PhD, as I am concerned about the time limit, given that all the other projects obviously have priority.

With regard to the work with my Australian collaborator, that has sped up! As said before, she now doesn't have to teach and we're making strides forward, so this is all really exciting. We took on another author on one of our projects, because they are an expert and it made sense. This project, on leadership, is now running parallel to a project on associative reasoning. We're also in the process of editing a book, so lots of good stuff going on there!

On the topic of teaching, I taught this term as well, although I remember saying that I wouldn't. I taught Strategic Games, which is just game theory. I really enjoyed the first five weeks, it gave me the structure I needed. It also made me feel useful as at least the students were benefiting from my work. However, I started to have issues of feeling overwhelmed around week 6 (half term) as my 50+-hour work weeks were getting to me (surprise). The irony is, I do think the fact that I "went hard", also known as working at least 50 hours a week on nothing but the PhD helped. I'm not saying it's healthy, because it isn't. I didn't even last 8 weeks doing that, but it did get me in a much better place with my work and supervisors. So do what you will with that information.

It probably requires explaining that this (over)working was simply being driven by the imposter syndrome, a fear of failing, a fear of never being good enough and the fact that the PhD just doesn't come with moments where someone looks at your finished work and says: "well done". The PhD is incredibly void of those moments.

If you take that gaping void and add it to doing job searches and applications which take up a lot of time, for little to no gain: I'm applying to jobs

I have no real interest in out of the sheer fear of unemployment and it's just raining rejections over here. You're just eating away at your own foundation of self-esteem, and that is just rough. "Just rough" is actually a pretty good way of describing this term.

To end this term: in the morning of the 22nd of March, I had my completion review during which there was the general agreement that I was on the right track and should be able to complete the PhD successfully. Hearing that one sentence was amazing. But it was immediately followed by 600 things I should still look at and improve. I lost most of my motivation of that week. As I'm writing this, we're still in that week. I have decided that it's time I take a much-needed break, because my resilience has dropped below zero.

Me writing this is reliving some of the worst parts. I cannot imagine that this makes for an interesting or even enjoyable read. Let's just hope the third term is better. Better can take many forms by this stage.

Term 3

I read back over my review of terms 1 and 2, what a depressing period that was. Well, I can tell you now, term 3 is less depressing, because quite frankly, I didn't feel anything.

I'm writing this on the 30th of June, which is the last week of term 3. I can summarize my progress with regard to the PhD chapters rather quickly.

Chapter 1 needed an additional study run, which literally finished running today. It'll take me at least a week to actually get the data into a shape in which it can be analyzed, but it also means there are no further experiments to run and that this is the last effort for the r&r (except rewriting it). Score!

Chapters 2 and 3 which I mentioned before as only requiring writing edits, well, that turned out to be a blatant lie. After my supervisors went over the text they decided that they didn't agree with some of the variables or results, which they had seen at least 10 times by that stage. So that required redoing. This only recently became an issue. This is very much going to be the type of thing I keep editing and adjusting until we're simply out of time. The main reason for this is that the data really aren't that great as they were hyped up to be. As a result of this, we also decided these chapters wouldn't be published. Which was both a relief and a slap to the face. As most things seem to be in the PhD.

The fourth chapter is finished as I was able to go through the counter-intuitive results with the help from my supervisors rather quickly. We know why those results are there, as peculiar as they may be. That chapter will also go through the editing phase now. The lucky thing with experimental data is that you cannot keep picking at it in the same way that you can with enormous amounts of third-party data.

The fifth chapter is also taking form, however, I only have 3 months left in the PhD, and we're still in the data checking and cleaning stage. It's very unlikely that this will make it into the PhD. Given the quality of the data, however, the work is very likely to be publishable, so I'll continue working on that after the PhD.

Arguably, that's everything going on for the PhD itself. Reading it like this it seems like rather little progress was made, but I can promise you lots of progress was actually made. I will submit on time, and that's all that matters.

In terms of the out-of-PhD work such as the Australian collaborations and projects, I have no clue what's happening there, as a lot of meetings just keep getting perpetually canceled. So over the third term, there were a negligible amount of meetings. Not my fault is all I can say to that.

Last, the job search and hunt has yielded some progress, with applications actually moving into the interview stages. I will keep you posted on progress there. I hope to have a job offer before I submit the thesis. Think of me!

As I mentioned in the beginning, this term I didn't really feel anything. There was no anxiety, or depression or any of the dread really associated with the end of the PhD. I think the reason I didn't feel much in this term is because the end is in sight, and I just want to be done with it. My only motivation is finishing in time and moving on with my life. I have mentally already checked out of the PhD. It happens.

Summer term

As you might have gathered from my writing over the years, the PhD working hours don't follow those of the actual term time. We don't take breaks when taught students do. So the summer term, especially the summer term of the final year, is actually quite stressful. It did not help I also had to move during this term. I decided to move back home and finish the PhD there, which I do think helped, a lot.

What was true in term 3 is still true now. Chapter 1 is part of a revise and resubmit and is taking up shape now. Our initial deadline was the 3rd of September, which was perfectly reasonable as it was our second extension. However, my supervisors cannot agree on the approach to the revision. And their visions are in direct conflict with each other: keep it as short as possible vs. working with more stuff that now needs to fit in the paper. So we have asked for yet another extension, now the 3rd of December. It's so abnormally slow… But I do think I'm getting there, and we might actually make the December deadline. It's just very frustrating to work on something for weeks straight, make massive edits and then be told in the supervisory meeting of 50 minutes that it isn't any good. Honestly, I received documents with edits where just entire pages are endless paragraphs of red text. Rinse and repeat.

Chapters 2, 3 and 4 are in the text-editing stage. As I said before, they will be edited until we run out of time. I genuinely believe that. After a suggestion at SPUDM (conference), I did play around with some of the data for Chapters 2 and 3 some more and found a way for explaining where all the money is coming from (quite important if you look at spending!) which might make the chapters publishable again. At least, one of my supervisors seems very keen on looking at that again, but that's for something after I submit and have had a break.

This summer term I do feel like I've gotten things done. I even took a bit of a break (I went to the seaside province, Zeeland), because my supervisors were on holiday and I couldn't do much without actual feedback.

In terms of the out-of-PhD work such as the collaborations and other projects, my collaborator has gotten back to me and we're back on track there. The "fifth" chapter is moving into the pre-registration stage, which is half the battle won. Both of these things will continue long after I submit the thesis, which is something I also want to write a post about: the fact that after the thesis submission the work really isn't done. Stay tuned for that!

Last, the job search. Have been made a job offer (!!!) and we're now in the stage of applying for visas, so I'm super excited! It took a while to get there, but I'm super eager to start the job as it's with a great company and great people, in the field I love. For those who are wondering, yes, I am leaving academia. Not my cup of tea, at least not for now.

Conclusions and announcements

If I had to describe the terms of this year, I would argue that term 1 was disillusionment, term 2 was pure panic, term 3 was "just get on with it" and the summer term was me trying to keep it all together before being #PhDone!

But now I am #PhDone. I have submitted. The beast was over 60,000 words and 188 pages. I am proud of it.

Going back over the blogs I've written regarding the PhD, the Questioning Behaviour episodes I recorded with Sarah focusing on people who have done the PhD and are now Early Career Researchers, and all the comments and questions I get from my readers about doing a PhD have lead me to the following announcement: I am going to write a book. I am going to write an entire guide about doing the PhD, from before its very start, the conception of the idea to do a PhD, to way after you submit, looking at vivas, job market tribulations and career switches. I think the book is necessary and I think academia has remained untransparent for long enough. So look forward to it!

And I did manage to write this book!

Things I Would Have Done Differently

The sole aim of this book is to give you (hopefully good) advice on how to make the most of your PhD experience. As you've gathered from the advice, contrasted to my own experiences, I'm one of those hypocrites who doesn't follow advice herself. So really, this chapter shouldn't be much of a surprise to you. After 4 years of doing a PhD, it's time I look back and reflect on the process and be honest with both myself and you, dear reader, in what I would've done differently, knowing what I know now.

Let's start at the very start, Section 1 material, I went into the PhD with a rather odd motivation: I had several awful job interviews for industry positions and, as a result, wrote the entirety of "behavioral science industry" off as a valid option. Obviously, as far as motivations for doing a PhD go, this one is really not that great. Doing a PhD is several years of dedication, opportunity cost and working in a rather untransparent system. You're better off having a more grounded and less delusional motivation than mine.

What would I have done differently? I should not have discarded all of industry. I should have researched alternatives to those specific companies better. I should have considered many more alternatives to doing a PhD. This book contains an entire section on good motivations to do a PhD, as well as bad motivations to do a PhD. Make sure you read this section carefully if you're trying to figure out whether a PhD is something for you!

In addition to doing more research on the alternatives in industry itself, I feel like I should have done more research on what a PhD program would be like. I was convinced I would spend 4 years (UK system) doing nothing but research, publishing throughout my journey and coming out of the PhD as a researcher extraordinaire. That did not happen.

Section 1 also contains a chapter on the misconceptions about doing a PhD in behavioral science, in which friends and colleagues outlined what they thought about doing a PhD before and after they were actually enrolled in the program. These two views are worlds apart. Again, my advice here is to do more research. Talk to alumni about the programs and universities you are interested in. Talk to the current supervisees (PhD students) of professors you are interested in having as a supervisor. This all helps in aligning your expectations with reality.

Talking about supervisors: I have also dedicated several chapters to this specific topic, because, and I'll say this time and time again: your supervisor can make or break your PhD. So you need to approach this strategically.

You can try looking for really well-published, famous and very busy professors but quite often these are not the best supervisors. I chose two of my MSc teachers to supervise me as they had a skillset I was lacking and I already knew them as people. At least I thought I did. Having someone as a teacher is not the same as having them as a supervisor and working towards publications together. Again, do your research. Best way of going about that in this case? Talk to their current and past supervisees (the PhD students they have already supervised). Ask targeted questions about the supervisors' workstyles, personalities, agreeability, professionalism, understanding, empathy, etc. You might have found out this way that the perceptions you held of someone were very far from the truth. It happens. Often, highly ranked academics have an inner and outer persona. Figure out which one you can and cannot work with.

In addition to doing more research, it might also help if you figure out early on what you want from the PhD. A PhD is a program designed to turn you into an independent researcher, an expert in a specific topic and place you on the lowest rung of the ladder leading into the pyramid scheme that is academia. These things are in that order, and that order only.

You can come out of a PhD being fully disillusioned about academia. The academic scene might simply be too slow for you, or too convoluted, or just not be a match for who you are and what your goals are as a person. In that case, you're now going to have to sell yourself into industry. It's less hard than you think, it just requires a completely different approach to what you have already been doing. People keep saying that industry "looks for different things", but a good independent researcher is a good independent researcher at the end of the day. Just make sure that you hit the right marketing key points for industry rather than academia. Often they "just" require rephrasing and restructuring. The CV is a bit different too!

If you knew about not wanting to stay in academia from the get-go, you had a lot more time figuring out how to sell yourself to industry. In fact, friends and colleagues of mine have designed their PhD programs and research cores to fit industry profiles, meaning they didn't really struggle that much in their "transition" into industry. If you have this as a head start, use it! However, I do ask you to consider whether doing a PhD is the best way of going about this: if your goal isn't academia, what is your motivation for doing a PhD? And are you sure there aren't any better alternatives?

I went wrong here as well. I was somehow convinced I would stay in academia, even though the PhD process and I weren't particularly compatible. If you read through my annual PhD reviews (years 1–4), you can just read the mismatch between the lines, especially in years 2 and 4. I should have been more honest with myself from the start and not have given into the sunk cost fallacy: just because I had started out working on the lowest rung launching me into the academic world, did not mean that's the only route I had available to me.

In the final year of the PhD, you will have to do a boat load of job applications. Can't be resting on your laurels now! So what did I do? I applied to doing post-docs, whereas I had already (sort of) come to terms with the idea of academia not being my cup of tea. The PhD environment prepares you for nothing else. Your supervisor(s), for obvious reasons, have little to no experience with going into industry. But just because the experience isn't directly surrounding you, doesn't mean you shouldn't seek it out. There are plenty of people who have done a PhD and then said "sayonara!" to academia. There are entire Twitter pages dedicated to them, I do recommend you follow them! #AltAc (alternatives to academia) opened up a wealth of information for me. And I'm sure it'll do the same for you.

What would I have done differently in my PhD? Overall, I should have done a lot more research. I don't think it would have changed too much about me ending up in Warwick, working with the two supervisors that I did work with. However, it would have changed how I approached the PhD and my perceptions of what it meant to be a successful PhD student, as well as a good researcher. It would have saved me from a lot of mental health strains, as well as my stubborn delusions about "needing" to become an academic. I'm not going to become an academic, because quite frankly, I don't want to.

If I had acknowledged my desire to leave academia earlier, I could have designed the PhD differently. In all fairness, thanks to my supervisor, most of my PhD was an analysis of third-party data, on a topic which is relevant for industry. However, I think it would have been good for me if I chased my own data earlier (I did so in the end!) and made more connections across industry, focusing on the research collaboration aspect. I think it would've been good for me.

And quite frankly, now that I'm writing this book, I wish I had taken up my own advice about enjoying the PhD more and the learning process it could have been. In hindsight I should've taken more classes in high-level coding and programming. In my field, and in many other fields, these are skills for life. I also should've had a research visit. Even though I did try to plan for one (I would've really enjoyed visiting Dilip Soman and BEAR at the University of Toronto), the pandemic ended up screwing that up for me. Unforeseen things always happen, unfortunate but true.

Last, I think I should have celebrated more. I'm a bit of a workaholic. I enjoy my work, at least most aspects of it. But what this leads to is that rather than looking at my progress and patting myself on the back is that I end up looking at everything else that still needs to happen and continue to grind away until all of it is done. At least for that specific project. And then I move onto the next project.

As I've outlined in the previous chapters on mental health, not taking a break, not taking a breath, not taking perspective, and not deriving a sense of achievement or even reward from finishing tasks can be a severe detriment to your own wellbeing. As I'm partially trained as a psychologist, I knew this. And I should've applied it to myself. I think I sometimes worked at my PhD so hard and was so overwhelmed with both determination and fear that I forgot to actually enjoy myself. And that makes me sad. I hope you can manage to do better.

And that's all there is to it. If you are thinking about doing a PhD, please do your research! Also, feel free to reach out if you have any questions. If you are doing/have done a PhD, what advice would you give? What would you have done differently? I'd love to hear it!

Concluding Remarks

How ironic is it that I'm using a blogpost to announce me writing a book about the PhD process, which is then published, months later, as a chapter in this book about the PhD process?

All jokes aside, may I congratulate you on finishing and submitting your PhD? This is an amazing feat and should be treated as such. Please go celebrate, in whichever way you want to, and in whichever way you can. If there's one thing I've learned and should've done much more myself, it's to celebrate your achievements. And this is one hell of an achievement.

If you're reading this book ahead of, or even during your PhD, but you haven't reached this stage yet, don't worry, it'll come. Granted that you don't endlessly faff about with small edits in your PhD. Honestly, submit already!

You'd think that after having finished the PhD, this book should end, but it doesn't. There's an entire next section coming about what happens after you're #PhDone. Because trust me, after you've just gone through this entire process, you're going to need some aftercare.

Section 6

PhDone! Now What?

So here we are. Submitted. Years of work have culminated into this very moment. How does it feel?

In the previous section, I mentioned the feelings that might arise from the actual act of submission. Pressing a button that makes you lose your online document to another dimension or actually having to hand a physical copy in. Dread, anxiety, relief and achievement, maybe even a hint of pride? Wonderful, isn't it?

As wonderful as it may, or may not, have been, these feelings are of rather short duration. So make sure you celebrate this milestone! Because life just has a nasty way of knocking you back to reality. And reality simply isn't different celebrations linked to each other. Unfortunately.

This section of the guide is about what comes after you submit, because, ironically enough, the work isn't done. In the next chapter, we'll discuss what work still needs to happen: you might want to still publish some papers, whether you continue in academia or not. There should (hopefully) also be time for a break — but there isn't always. Your mental health may also need some looking after. And potentially, your hunt for a job continues. All of this will be discussed in this section. Let's start with the anti-climax of submitting!

The Anti-Climax of Submitting

You've submitted your thesis. The PhD thesis, that is. Congratulations! You must feel very accomplished or at least very relieved right now. I know I did.

Of course, you have now more than deserved taking a break. A long break. Time to relax and read the books you wanted to still read (preferably not work related). See some friends and family you haven't seen in a while. Be social. Be merry. Be free. And then get back to it!

Back to it?! Yes, my friend, back to it. Although you might be done with the PhD, it remains to be seen whether the PhD is done with you. Let me explain.

When it comes to exiting (read: finishing) a PhD, there are about two roads out of it. You either stay in academia, moving into a post-doc (or an assistant professorship if you're lucky!) or you leave academia. The latter is known as moving into industry, although arguably, academia is an industry.

Now if you stay in academia, a large chunk of your worth is determined by the research you do, whether that research is publishable and, obviously, whether it has been published. So once you submit the dissertation, you'll still need to convert the chapters into publishable papers.

A chapter does not equal a paper ready for peer-reviewed publication.

It absolutely does not.

A PhD dissertation, although it may have chapters in there that have been tailored to fit certain journals, have already received revises and resubmits, or, have already been published, is not often of publishable quality (yet). This does differ per program. In economics, each PhD candidate needs a "job market paper" which is essentially one of their chapters that has been edited to the journal standard already. But that doesn't mean the rest of the dissertation is of this quality as well (at least, not yet). In programs which are longer than the UK programs, say the US programs, there is more time for this type of editing, so often publishing is much more expected within these programs. Just so you know.

It is also possible that you're in a field that puts much more emphasis on collaboration (economics is not one of those), like physics. Or in general, the natural sciences. In the Netherlands, graduating from a PhD in physics warrants that you have three of your chapters published as peer-reviewed papers and have another one in the pipeline. The lucky thing here is that you will have an entire team of collaborators/co-authors, so this is actually doable.

Whichever field and program you may have found yourself in, not all of your dissertation will be of publishable quality, yet. As I said, if you want to stay in academia and find yourself in a post-doc (or higher) you have essentially found yourself on a continuation of your PhD, against higher pay (at least I hope so). You can continue to edit your chapters until they are of journal quality and submit them for review and hopefully get publications out of them. Depending on your field, this can take months to years. So the work isn't exactly done.

The fact that the work isn't done is not so much of an issue if you stay in academia, as this is essentially a continuation of your research. If you're leaving academia, however, this may be a much larger problem. Working on your PhD research will very likely not be considered part of your industry job and will fall into the remit of "extracurricular activities", meaning outside of your 9–5.

Whether you still want to publish having moved into industry is, as a result, entirely up to you. Some people still see the value in it. Others just suffer the sunk cost fallacy. I know I subscribe to both viewpoints.

I'm mainly bringing up this point as turning a chapter into a paper is a very hefty and long process, for which you will require constant input from your supervisors, now essentially colleagues, who have more experience doing this. It can take months and months and months. So if you do want to publish and your PhD has been submitted, well, prepare for a lot more work that is still related to your PhD. Submission may have felt very final, but it really doesn't have to be.

Of course, if you don't find any value in publishing any of your chapters and just want to be done with it, no one can force you to publish!

Regardless of which of the two roads you choose, a PhD isn't finished when you submit. You don't just submit a PhD and wash your hands of it. There is also the defense of the dissertation. Often referred to as the viva. Keep in mind that this is also work. Although it may not be as much work as it sounds.

Depending on your program the viva can take many forms. It can be you giving a presentation on your chapters: motivation, methods, results and contributions. Those four points really need to be hit and you're essentially good from thereon. After the presentation, you'll very likely have a critical discussion with several examiners and Bob's your uncle. Obviously, the work for this form of viva is to make a great presentation and do a lot of editing on this one as well.

It can also be a much more chill affair. The approach at my university is to have just a discussion about the thesis, as the examiners have read it carefully and very often don't require a recap. In this case, you sit down (often in a room, currently online) and get questions about the work, the work's context and your contributions to the field. My supervisors recommended that I reread my own thesis about a week before the viva itself and that should do it. Not that much work.

Given the wide range of options that vivas can have, I've dedicated an entire chapter (Chapter 47) to it. So don't worry, it's coming!

Leaving the viva and the publishing aside, there is an often hidden work obligation during and sometimes after the PhD that doesn't get much of a mention, and that's the job hunt. Being on the job market is very often not that easy, and in the past year and a bit, thanks to the pandemic, a lot of people have really struggled.

When staying in academia, you can start applying to post-docs about 1 year before the post-doc is supposed to start (and your PhD is supposed to end). That means that from the start of your final year onwards, job applications will become your extracurricular activity. This takes up a lot of time. Don't underestimate this, it will take up a lot of time.

Now, this time can be shortened by not just applying "willy-nilly" but doing a much more targeted set of applications to research groups that you know and know you. This requires a lot of networking during your PhD — another hidden work cost — and a really important one at that!

If you haven't done this type of networking, then you'll be dealing with "cold" applications, and then it becomes a numbers game. The success rate for these is much lower, which means it'll take more and more time. This can happen both during and after the PhD.

When leaving academia and transitioning "into industry", the turnaround is very different. Industry jobs don't expect to wait 12 months, they expect to wait approximately 3 months (on average, these numbers aren't gospel). Despite the temporal difference, the same rules apply. If you haven't networked and found yourself "an in", this will again be a numbers game.

Often PhD candidates apply to both types of jobs as the time horizon is so very different. One thing to keep in mind: an academic CV is not the same as an industry CV, so read what the job entails very carefully and edit your documents accordingly. Again, this will cost time.

I didn't write this chapter to scare people off. I think if you're reading this, you're probably already in a PhD, so the scare would be a bit too late anyway. I'm just trying to highlight the choices you have and which paths these choices might take you down in terms of work that has to happen after the PhD. Also, I cannot emphasize this enough but network. Networking, setting up contacts and collaborations at research groups, universities and organizations that do similar work to yours is always a good idea. Trust me.

Now having said that there's still a lot of work to be done, I do recommend you take a break. It's almost ironic, isn't it?

The Break?!

The work never really ends, but you should take breaks regardless of the heap of work still looking at you. Submitting the PhD thesis may feel anticlimactic as you're (now) aware of the mountain of work that still needs to happen, but still, a break is in order.

From a mental health perspective, celebrating this massive milestone with a break is a very good idea. It doesn't matter how small or big you celebrate this feat. Maybe you take a week off. Just lounge about in your own home. Don't move. Eat copious amounts of pizza which no nutritionist would recommend you do. Maybe you go back home to your family for several weeks or months. Especially international students might want to consider this, because during the last stretch of your PhD, you often do neglect them a bit (I know this, I've done this). Maybe you don't want to be anywhere familiar. Maybe you want to book several weeks of a small world tour: discover all of Asia on a backpacking trip [it's really a basic bitch move (read: white middle-class), but if you want to, you go for it]. Who cares what you do, as long as you take a break!

Why am I pushing for a break so much? Well, without getting too biological (because I simply don't have the degrees to back this knowledge up), it's been a very stressful period for you. The PhD is a very stressful period. Even if you were cool as a cucumber throughout most of the process, there must have been times when even you wanted to throw your supervisor(s) or your equipment out of a window. Or just into a bin. Either will do really. You have been producing stress hormones (mainly cortisol) for a while now. The body cannot sustain long periods of cortisol production for very long, it comes at the expense of the production of other hormones and other processes that your body requires, such as good sleep (maintaining the circadian rhythm) and digestion. So taking a break, from a biological perspective, is imperative. You need to get back to homeostasis — the level your body wants to function at.

This increased cortisol production also plays tricks on the mind: it's essentially your body telling you that you're stressed (surprise!). I'm sure you could've figured this out without your body telling you, but it is what it is. A break will also allow you to take stock of the past years. What was good? What was bad? How have you grown as a researcher? How have you grown as a person? Do you now have a better idea of what you want? And don't want? I'm sure that if you give yourself the time to ponder these things, you'll notice a massive growth within yourself. And that's great. You do need to give yourself some time to recognize this though.

Now I also recognize that taking a break might be difficult for a variety of reasons:

1. it might not be financially feasible,
2. it might not be feasible with regard to work, or
3. it might not be mentally feasible.

Points 1 and 2 are rather entangled. As soon as you submit your PhD, your funding runs out. It doesn't matter that you still have work to do (e.g. continued research on publishing, the viva), it's likely that your institution doesn't really care about that. What people often do as a result is plan their next job straight after the submission deadline or even before it. I know of people (my mentors, friends and colleagues) taking up a post-doc (or equivalent) position *before* they even submitted their PhD thesis. Can you imagine?! What this means is that as soon as you submit, or even slightly before, you start the other job. Your hours get shifted to this job, and you are now fully employed. Often, when transitioning into a new job, the first thing you do is not going on holiday. For some reason that is frowned upon. But not nearly as much as you think. There are ways of still making this work: if you're staying in academia you can tell them to push back your starting date by a couple of days, so you at least get some days off where you can just lounge about. The academic system is rather flexible like that. And if you cannot take the holiday immediately, maybe in a couple weeks' or months' time? Get onto HR early about this one, it might make all the difference. For people leaving academia and moving into industry do the same thing. No joke, just check with HR or your new boss whether they're happy to delay your starting date by a few days or a full week. Have a small break. This type of break shouldn't impact your financial situation too much and does tie you over, allowing you to reset your system a bit. And take a larger break later, whenever works for the team roster.

It's also possible, coming back to point 2, that you've done the PhD part-time, while holding down a different job at the same time. As a result, the financial aspect should be less pressing, but the time component still plays a large role. The lucky thing here is, you've already built some serious credit with this company and have shown them to be a dedicated employee over the time span of a minimum of 5 years (probably a lot more). You know your submission date way ahead of time, so you can just roll up to HR (or your line manager, depends on the company) and book the week(s) after your thesis submission off. Maybe even book off the week before submission. Who knows?

Moving onto point 3, you're not mentally comfortable with the idea of a break. The idea of having to just "be idle" after years of pushing through is just not appealing to you. Maybe being idle has simply never been appealing to you. I know people like this, and I am like this as well. The joke of being called a workaholic, especially if it's true, loses its appeal fairly quickly, but it is what it is. To ease yourself into the idea of a break, if there's one thing I know about workaholics, is that they have a little list (either in their head, or written down somewhere), which contains a number of things they still wanted to do or learn. Why don't you ease into a break by crossing some things off that list? After my submission, there were several places in Europe I still wanted to see before I moved to Australia, so I went to visit those. If that's too "holiday-esque" for you, learn a new skill. I learned audio-editing for the Questioning Behaviour Podcast which I co-host. I think I'll dive into Photoshop and video editing next. Maybe even start a new project, which is not affiliated with your PhD research. I started writing this guide. It's PhD affiliated, I'll give you that, but not related to my actual research, so I really enjoyed the writing process.

A break doesn't need to be lying on a beach with nothing but your thoughts (I know, scary). It can be anything: learning new things, spending entire nights gaming without restrictions, finishing every book in a library, climbing Kilimanjaro, going to see your family, etc. It's all good. And maybe, you don't want the break at all. It sounds a bit masochistic but I knew people who were just so "over" the PhD and wanted to dive into something else. That's fair too. Their break was to just break away from the PhD. Fair play.

The only thing I can say about having a break, however short or intense it may be, is that it really helps if you can give yourself the time to reflect upon an important life experience, see what you've learned and how you've grown and what you want to do with it. Take stock, shift your perspective from being a person doing a PhD to a person who has done a PhD and go from there. No beach involved!

The Viva

Whether you've taken a break or not, eventually, the day will come that you will have to defend your thesis. I'll be honest, I was wary about writing this chapter, because the viva can come in many shapes and sizes.

In my case, the viva was a very chill affair. A minimum of 6 weeks after your PhD thesis submission, your viva will be scheduled (in my case 9 weeks after). This viva was being done online thanks to the pandemic (November 2021) and was scheduled to last 3 hours maximum. In those 3 hours, I did not have to present, I was simply asked questions about my research, my contributions to the field, etc. by the internal and external examiners — there were only two of them. Nothing new, nothing to be worried about. All in all, quite a chill conversation. I enjoyed it. After we had the 3-hour conversation, the examiners told me the amount of corrections required and when to do them by. That was it.

This is not the normal experience that most people have when doing a viva or any form of thesis defense. Normally, it's a lot more intense than this. Let me explain. Friends of mine who have done their PhD in the Netherlands had two different vivas. One of them was private, resembling the one above, but with more people present, and they had a public viva as well. In the private one, the examiners had read the thesis beforehand (as they also had in mine), watch the student present the thesis to them (which can take up to an hour) and then ask the student questions about their work. This can be grueling but doesn't last for 3 hours as seen with mine. It's more likely to take another hour. After this, the examiners will tell the PhD student what corrections are required and by when they are required. After the student has done these corrections, has resubmitted and these corrections have been accepted, the public viva is scheduled. This public viva is an event. Several bigwigs of the university have to show up to hear you present. Everyone is in their robes. There is a man with a staff present knocking it onto the floor to indicate the start and end of the presentation and the event as a whole. It's very formal. And public. You can invite your family, friends and co-workers, anyone is welcome. Some people even had press present. Now some people may find this mortifying or just plain ridiculous, but the thing is, this presentation is both formal and a formality. Once your corrections are accepted, that's it — the PhD degree is in the pocket. This really is just an event to celebrate the achievements of the PhD student and showcase their hard work. I personally would've loved to have a public viva. Alas.

It depends on your field, department, university or maybe even country, what form of viva you're going to have. This is why I was wary to write this chapter: there's a lot of variability in what it means to do a viva. The only advice I can really give is to ask your supervisor(s) about this early on — start of your final year maybe? And talk it through with colleagues and friends that have already been through this process. Another thing you might want to ask your friends and colleagues: how should you prepare?

However chill my experience was, you can't just rock up to the viva and hope for the best. Preparing for the viva starts a bit earlier than you think. In my case, a month before submission, the department wanted an official-looking document stating my choice of internal and external examiners, as well as the meeting chair. You can't just write down three random names and hope for the best. I mean, you could, but it's a terrible idea. The idea is that you reach out to both the internal and the external examiner way before to have them confirm that they're happy to do this for you. Preferably, your supervisor(s) helps you select these examiners. The reason for this is simple: they'll know these people and may have some experience with them. The last thing you want at your viva is to present your work to an esteemed colleague who turns out to be a nasty piece of work, ruining your experience and making you do many more corrections to your PhD than anyone else would have made you do. Your supervisor(s) should be "in the know" about who's good and who isn't. At least in terms of (external) examiners. Keep in mind, your (external) examiner is required to be an expert in your PhD topic. My examiners were chosen by my supervisors and I was okay with their choices.

It is also possible that your meeting chair (also referred to as "promotor") was set from the get-go as you enrolled in the PhD program (e.g. they're the head of the group that you're with, but not your direct supervisor). It's also possible that you have to present in front of the entire research group and all those with tenure determine whether you're good to go or not. Again, there's too much variability here for me to make any real comments — make sure you ask those who do know what you're up for.

Regardless of the viva format, the bare minimum of preparation required for it is to re-read your thesis. Maybe you've had a break, chilling on the beach, or maybe you've jumped straight into a new job working the day away. Either way, it's been a while since you've looked at this document. The start is to re-read it and get reacquainted.

While you're reading, you may also want to take notes. A quick summary or bullet points on important literature, your methods, results, limitations, contributions (this one is very important!) and further research required. It is really important to be able to correctly articulate the value added by your PhD to the research already done. So if you want to write that down and practice that, no one is going to stop you. I actually think it's quite a good idea!

If your viva requires you to present your work, you might want to start this presentation a bit earlier as well (meaning, not a week before the viva). Why? So your supervisor(s) can look it over and give you pointers. Now, the content of the presentation shouldn't be changing too much, if at all, as the thesis has been submitted. You may have continued working on the research, and you can mention this during the presentation, but you have to be very careful doing this — they haven't read this new work, because, well, they couldn't have. That's not the work you provided them with. Your supervisor(s) should mainly be giving you pointers on the presentation flow and what points to really emphasize during the presentation. It's your first time, not theirs.

Now, let's assume you've done the viva. What happens now is that you get corrections. You've heard the term before, but I think it warrants some more explanation. In the UK, but in most other systems as well, there are only four possible outcomes: no corrections, minor corrections, major corrections or a fail. Let's discuss them in turn.

To receive no corrections on a PhD thesis means the work is of such high quality it could get immediately published in high-level journals in that field, no further edits required. This doesn't mean the work needs to have been published already. If you receive this, good for you! This also means you don't need to resubmit your thesis — it's good as it is. You can call yourself doctor now!

To receive minor corrections on a PhD thesis means the work is of such high quality it could get published in high-level journals in that field, with minor edits required. These edits can be as minor as correcting typos, changing sentence structures or changing graph axes. Or the edits can be a bit less minor, requiring more effort by incorporating some more references in your literature review or expanding your discussion section to also encompass a different line of thought/theory. However, the latter is a lot less likely. Receiving this is a very good outcome. A close friend of mine received this outcome for his PhD and banged the minor edits out in an afternoon. Like I said, they're minor! After those edits have been done, you resubmit the thesis and it gets checked over again by the examiners to determine whether the corrections were sufficient, and once approved, you can call yourself doctor!

To receive major corrections on a PhD thesis means the work is of sufficient quality it could get published in journals in that field but requires major edits to make this happen. These edits can take on a variety of forms, and all of them will require a lot more work. This can be the conducting of additional studies or the rewriting of your entire literature review to incorporate a lot more prior work or to position your theories or arguments completely differently. Often, if you have to redo the literature review your arguments or hypotheses are based on, you'll also have to redo your discussion section(s), as one flows from the other. This is not a good outcome, and quite frankly, your supervisor(s) should have prevented this from occurring. If they didn't think you could get through a viva without major corrections, they shouldn't have let you submit to begin with, and you should have had discussions about extensions. Probably you should have had discussions about the quality of the work way before this stage, and issues like this should have come up during annual reviews. Major corrections, unsurprisingly, cannot be banged out in an afternoon. They will be days and more likely weeks or even months of additional work, depending on how much time you can spare. After you've managed to do these major corrections, you again resubmit and the work gets checked again. It's entirely possible that the edits are so major that you will be asked to present again. It's not likely, but it's possible.

Worse than major corrections, which do occur, don't get me wrong, is to fail the viva completely. In this case, your board of examiners, or whomever you're presenting to, do not deem this work as being remotely of high enough quality to be published or even salvageable. What you have submitted is below standard and cannot pass. It's possible that your work is deemed of low quality (not scientifically robust), not sufficient (too small sample sizes, too few experiments, not enough development of theoretical concepts, no real individual contribution to prior work, etc.) or not yours. In the latter case, the examiners doubt whether you have actually contributed enough to your own thesis to call it *your* work. Again, if something like this happens, you need to have a serious chat with your supervisor(s) or maybe even the department and HR, as your supervisor(s) never should have let you submit if the work was of such low quality. I'm pretty sure we had a printout of an article hanging by our PhD office printer detailing how a PhD student who failed their viva had sued their university as a result of this. I'm just saying that a PhD dissertation doesn't just reflect the intellectual value of the PhD student, but it also shines a light on the input of the supervisor(s). Enough said.

These are the four options that most systems aim for. In some systems, you can also get a grade for your PhD thesis, which quite frankly, I find odd. This grade may still entail corrections are warranted, but it may not. The best thing here is to, again, ask those who are in the know!

I think having discussed the preparation, possible formats and possible outcomes of the viva, I am happy in closing this chapter. Maybe one piece of advice to end on: don't stress about this too much, enjoy it! This is going to be a presentation or a conversation about *your* work. *Your* research. *You* are the expert, have your moment in the spotlight and enjoy it.

Concluding Remarks: The Aftermath

It took me a while to figure out what to name this chapter. What do you name a chapter which is supposed to describe everything when it's all said, done and submitted? After the viva and the corrections, that is it. You're done. You can call yourself doctor. You can go to your graduation ceremony (if you feel so inclined, I missed mine. Despite it being online, it was still during UK working hours and I had already moved to Australia by then). Take all the selfies. Take all the breaks. Celebrate and reward yourself endlessly. It's done.

It's also entirely possible that the aftermath also feels completely anti-climactic. It did for me. Between the submission and the graduation ceremony I had my next job lined up and was just waiting to get started. My break had become a bit longer than expected due to visa and traveling issues due to COVID. No biggie, but simply not exactly how I had expected things to go.

In addition to the break being longer than expected, it wasn't a full break either. I continued working for a large part of it. I did take a month off after submission, but as soon as that month had passed, I started getting back to work affiliated with the PhD. In my case, this was resubmitting an r&r and shaping the pre-registration for a research project that I started during the PhD but paused when the deadline of the actual PhD came closer and closer. This project is still in collaboration with my supervisors, making the "end" of the PhD even more anti-climactic. In addition to this, one of my other collaborators came out of the woodwork again as her teaching term had ended, and we could go back to our research which will entail meetings over the December–January period to get a book and two papers published. We keep busy.

I also took 2 weeks off immediately after my viva. I finally started taking my own advice about celebrating, taking breaks and recharging. Better late than never right?

I cannot tell you what the aftermath will be like for you. You might have hopped straight onto your next job, whether that's in academia or not. You might have decided to take a break before you start your next job, like I did. It's also possible you're still looking for jobs. I hope that I have outlined how to best go about finding a job, in academia and/or industry in the previous sections. I do wish you the best of luck.

Whether you immediately find a job after your PhD is also not a reflection of how good you are as a person or as a researcher. It really isn't. I know I keep hammering the mental health message home, but some of this stuff, if not all of this stuff, is a reflection of the system rather than you. You're not a PhD student, you are doing a PhD. You are not a failure, one aspect (or multiple) of your PhD went wrong. You are capable and you can do this. And once you're at the end of this book, well guess what? You have done this. Job hunting is not a great process, especially not if you're facing a lot of rejections or just a lack of replies, but you'll get there eventually. Trust the process. Or rather, trust yourself to make it work.

Keep in mind that the aftermath, as I so ominously called it, is not the first few weeks after you submitted and defended your PhD. It's the whole of your career and life after it. What you do with the lessons you learned during the PhD is up to you. If it was one of the best times of your career/life, good for you! If it was one of the worst, I'm sorry. It unfortunately does happen. And it has happened. Take what you can from it and move on. Move onto better and more amazing things!

Conclusion

I started this book off explaining why I wrote it: to help others who had reached out to me with their questions. I received a broad range of questions: Should I do a PhD? Do I need to do a PhD? How do I find the right topic or the right supervisor? Do I need to go to the States for a PhD? And sometimes, even highly personal questions: I'm thinking about quitting my PhD after [specific incident], do you think that's wise? Truly, I've seen almost every question under the sun, and I've always tried my best to help. But I didn't think this was the most efficient way of reaching the vast amounts of people who I know have these questions.

If you've now gone through this whole book, you should have read close to 50 (!!!) chapters of my advice to you. The advice has been collected from my own experience, my friends' and colleagues' experiences, as well as stories shared online. There's a lot of information out there, but I thought it would be a good idea to collate it into a single guide. I hope it was a good idea.

To come back to you and your experience, I hope this book helped you. If you read the whole book before even starting your PhD, I hope the different sections were able to guide you through the decision-making process of doing a PhD, as well as applying to different institutions and maximizing your chances of getting a program of your choice. I hope it also prepared you for what's to come.

If you read this book when already in a PhD, I hope it helped you prepare for things that you may or may not encounter in the PhD itself. Or, if you had already encountered some of the things, it helps you deal with those things in a constructive way. It may also help you help others and normalize the discussion around some of these topics, such as feelings of failure, mental health or opening up about working relationships that may not be working. The PhD can be a very lonely experience, however, you do have a cohort. Try to support them if they're going through hardships, in the way that you would want them to support you. If you can stand together, you'll find that you're not nearly as alone as you thought you were. People stand taller together.

If you read this book when being close to finishing the PhD or even having finished the PhD, I hope you recognized some of your own experiences in it. I hope this book puts some of your experiences into perspective. Who knows? Maybe you'll even move on to becoming a PhD supervisor yourself — be kind to those you supervise. The PhD is a unique experience for each and every individual doing one, so be patient and try to truly understand their point of view.

And, less likely but still possible, if you've read through this entire guide to make up your mind about doing a PhD, don't be discouraged about all the chapters in Section 4! I know there are a lot of nightmare scenarios in there, but that's just because that's what people need advice about! I can't dedicate 50 odd chapters to describing how wonderful a PhD can be. Of course it can be a great experience. Even if you do run into issues as described in Section 4 or any of the other sections, that doesn't mean the PhD itself is a nightmare. There're just some possibilities that come with the terrain that need exploring. And you're best off knowing these things in advance.

Whichever of the above-described readers you are, I hope that when you've gone through your PhD and can call yourself Dr, you reflect on the experience with mainly positive emotions. Even if it's just a learning experience. I hope this book can help you to maximize the utility you can get out of the PhD program and succeed in whatever it is that you want to do afterwards.

Congratulations on finishing your PhD. Onto (even) better things!

www.ingramcontent.com/pod-product-compliance
Lightning Source LLC
Chambersburg PA
CBHW070308230426

43664CB00015B/2676